SPECTRUM

Test Prep

Grade 6

Published by Spectrum
an imprint of Carson-Dellosa Publishing LLC
Greensboro, NC

Spectrum
An imprint of Carson-Dellosa Publishing LLC
P.O. Box 35665
Greensboro, NC 27425 USA

ISBN 0-7696-8626-5

9 10 11 12 13 PAH 14 13 12 11   053118091

Table of Contents

What's Inside? 5

English Language Arts

Standards and What They Mean 7

Reading and Comprehension
Establishing a Purpose for Reading 9
Applying Appropriate Reading Strategies. . . 11
Identifying Genres 13
Identifying Unknown Words. 15
Using Context Clues. 16
Mini-Test 1 . . . . **17**

Writing
Using Nouns 18
Using Pronouns and Verbs 19
Subject and Verb Agreement 20
Simple and Compound Sentences 21
Writing with a Focus 22
Using Appropriate Content. 23
Identifying Point of View 24
Spelling and Capitalization 25
Punctuation 26
Using Figurative Language. 27
Mini-Test 2 . . . . **28**

Research
Locating Information in Texts. 29
Using Technological Resources 30
Mini-Test 3 . . . . **32**

Cultural and Social Language Use
Comparing Works from Different
    Times and Places. 33
Writing About Community 34
Writing to Communicate 35
Mini-Test 4 . . . . **36**

How Am I Doing? **37**

Final English Language Arts Test **39**
Answer Sheet 42

Mathematics

Standards and What They Mean 43

Number and Operations
Prime Factorization 44
Percents, Decimals, and Fractions 45
Percentages and Ratios 46
Using Inverse Relationships. 47
Order of Operations 48

Algebra
Generating Functions 49
Using Variables 50
Algebraic Expressions 51
Solving One-Step Equations. 52
Changing Dimensions 53
Mini-Test 1 . . . . **54**

Geometry
Classifying Quadrilaterals. 55
Classifying Polyhedrons. 56
Using a Coordinate System 57
Analyzing Transformations. 58
Rotational and Line Symmetry. 59
Finding the Volume of
    Three-Dimensional Models 60

Measurement
Identifying Equivalent Units of Measure. . . . 61
Circumference and Area of Circles 62
Finding the Measurement of
    Unknown Angles 63
Finding Perimeter, Area, and Volume 64
Mini-Test 2 . . . . **65**

Data Analysis and Probability
Using Stem and Leaf Plots. 66
Mean, Median, Mode, and Range. 67
Effect of Sample Size on Probabilities 68
Listing Outcomes. 69

Process
Solving Problems. 70
Using Mathematical Language. 71
Applying Math to Other Areas 72
Communicating Mathematical Ideas 73
Mini-Test 3 . . . . **74**

How Am I Doing? **75**

Final Mathematics Test. **76**
Answer Sheet 79

Social Studies

Standards and What They Mean **80**

Culture
    Cultural Diversity in the United States 81
    Comparing Cultural Characteristics 82

Time, Continuity, and Change
    Matching Events to Historical Stories 84
    Different Perspectives on
        Historical Events 85

People, Places, and Environment
    Using a Map 86
    Effect of Human Activity on
        the Environment 87
    Mini-Test 1 . . . . **88**

Individual Development and Identity
    Influences on Values 89
    Regional Influences on Identity 90

Individuals, Groups, and Institutions
    Major Religions of the World and
        the United States 91
    Social Changes in the Progressive Era 92
    Mini-Test 2 . . . . **93**

Powers, Authority, and Governance
    The Federal System in the United States . . . 94
    The President's Cabinet 95

Production, Distribution, and Consumption
    Identifying Economic Systems 96
    Public Goods and Services 98

Science, Technology, and Society
    Inventions That Changed Society 99
    Mini-Test 3 . . . . **100**

Global Connections
    How Trade Benefits Countries 101

Civic Ideals and Practices
    Freedom of Expression 103
    The Bill of Rights and Due
        Process of Law 104
    Mini-Test 4 . . . . **105**

How Am I Doing? **106**

Final Social Studies Test **108**
    Answer Sheet 111

Science

Standards and What They Mean **112**

Unifying Concepts and Processes
    Scientific Models and Patterns
        of Change 114
    Identifying Simple Systems 115

Science as Inquiry
    Making Scientific Observations 116
    Scientific Experiments 117
    Mini-Test 1 . . . . **118**

Physical Science
    Physical and Chemical Changes 119
    Changes in Physical Properties 120
    Force and Motion 121

Life Science
    Identifying Roles of Organisms 122
    Adaptive Characteristics 123

Earth and Space Science
    Characteristics of Earth and Moon 125
    Forces Within Earth 126
    Mini-Test 2 . . . . **127**

Science and Technology
    Conservation, Technology, and
        Ecosystems 128

Science in Personal and Social Perspectives
    Identifying Learned Traits 129

History and Nature of Science
    The Discoveries of Isaac Newton 130
    Mini-Test 3 . . . . **131**

How Am I Doing? **132**

Final Science Test **133**
    Answer Sheet 136

Answer Key **137**

What's Inside?

This workbook is designed to help you and your sixth grader understand what he or she will be expected to know on standardized tests.

Practice Pages

The workbook is divided into four sections: English Language Arts, Mathematics, Social Studies, and Science. The practice activities in this workbook provide students with practice in each of these areas. Each section has practice activities that have questions similar to those that will appear on the standardized tests. Students should use a pencil to fill in the correct answers and to complete any writing on these activities.

National Standards

Before each practice section is a list of the national standards covered by that section. These standards list the knowledge and skills that students are expected to master at each grade level. The shaded *What it means* sections will help to explain any information in the standards that might be unfamiliar.

Mini-Tests and Final Tests

When your student finishes the practice pages for specific standards, your student can move on to a mini-test that covers the material presented on those practice activities. After an entire set of standards and accompanying practice pages are completed, your student should take the final tests, which incorporates materials from all the practice pages in that section.

Final Test Answer Sheet

The final tests have a separate answer sheet that mimics the style of the answer sheets the students will use on the standardized tests. The answer sheets appear at the end of each final test.

How Am I Doing?

The *How Am I Doing?* pages are designed to help students identify areas where they are proficient and areas where they still need more practice. They will pinpoint areas where more work is needed as well as areas where your student excels. Students can keep track of each of their mini-test scores on these pages.

Answer Key

Answers to all the practice pages, mini-tests, and final tests are listed by page number and appear at the end of the book.

To find a complete listing of the national standards in each subject area, you can access the following Web sites:

The National Council of Teachers of English: www.ncte.org
National Council of Teachers of Mathematics: www.nctm.org/standards
National Council for the Social Studies: www.ncss.org/standards
National Science Teachers Association: www.nsta.org/standards

English Language Arts Standards

Standard 1 *(See pages 9–12.)*
Students read a wide range of print and nonprint texts to build an understanding of texts, of themselves, and of the cultures of the United States and the world; to acquire new information; to respond to the needs and demands of society and the workplace; and for personal fulfillment. Among these texts are fiction and nonfiction, classic and contemporary works.

Standard 2 *(See pages 13–14.)*
Students read a wide range of literature from many periods in many genres to build an understanding of the many dimensions (e.g., philosophical, ethical, aesthetic) of human experience.

Standard 3 *(See pages 15–16.)*
Students apply a wide range of strategies to comprehend, interpret, evaluate, and appreciate texts. They draw on their prior experience, their interactions with other readers and writers, their knowledge of word meaning and of other texts, their word identification strategies, and their understanding of textual features (e.g., sound-letter correspondence, sentence structure, context, graphics).

Standard 4 *(See pages 18–21.)*
Students adjust their use of spoken, written, and visual language (e.g., conventions, style, vocabulary) to communicate effectively with a variety of audiences and for different purposes.

Standard 5 *(See pages 22–24.)*
Students employ a wide range of strategies as they write and use different writing process elements appropriately to communicate with different audiences for a variety of purposes.

Standard 6 *(See pages 25–27.)*
Students apply knowledge of language structure, language conventions (e.g., spelling and punctuation), media techniques, figurative language, and genre to create, critique, and discuss print and nonprint texts.

Standard 7 *(See page 29.)*
Students conduct research on issues and interests by generating ideas and questions, and by posing problems. They gather, evaluate, and synthesize data from a variety of sources (e.g., print and nonprint texts, artifacts, people) to communicate their discoveries in ways that suit their purpose and audience.

Standard 8 *(See pages 30–31.)*
Students use a variety of technological and informational resources (e.g., libraries, databases, computer networks, video) to gather and synthesize information and to create and communicate knowledge.

Standard 9 *(See page 33.)*
Students develop an understanding of and respect for diversity in language use, patterns, and dialects across cultures, ethnic groups, geographic regions, and social roles.

English Language Arts Standards

Standard 10
Students whose first language is not English make use of their first language to develop competency in the English language arts and to develop understanding of content across the curriculum.

Standard 11 *(See page 34.)*
Students participate as knowledgeable, reflective, creative, and critical members of a variety of literacy communities.

Standard 12 *(See page 35.)*
Students use spoken, written, and visual language to accomplish their own purposes (e.g., for learning, enjoyment, persuasion, and the exchange of information).

Name _____   Date _____

English Language Arts

Establishing a Purpose for Reading
Reading and Comprehension

DIRECTIONS: Read the passage and then choose the best answer to each question.

Example:

The liver is the largest of the body's glands. It helps the body absorb food by producing a fluid that breaks down the food taken into the body. The liver clears the blood of many harmful products it can absorb. The liver also stores sugar for future use and makes sure that the heart does not become overloaded with blood.

How many functions does the liver perform?

(A) one

(B) two

(C) three

(D) four

Answer: (D)

The Ship of the Desert

Nomads who crisscross the Sahara Desert of North Africa rely on a most unique animal for transportation—the dromedary, or one-humped camel. Because it is indispensable to desert travel, the dromedary is sometimes called the *ship of the desert.*

Several factors make the dromedary suitable for long desert trips. It can go for long periods without nourishment. The hump on a camel's back serves as its food reserve. When it has little to eat, it converts the fat from its hump into energy. The camel's hump can weigh 80 pounds or more. When the animal has to rely on its reservoir of fat, the hump becomes much smaller. Thus, it is easy to recognize a well-fed camel by the size of its hump.

Many people believe that camels store water in their humps. This is not true. Their ability to go for days without drinking is due to other factors. First, camels are able to drink large quantities of water at one time. Some have been known to gulp 53 gallons in one day. Second, the camel sweats very little and can tolerate greater body temperatures. Consequently, it retains most of the water it drinks and can travel several hundred miles before replenishing its supply.

Other physical characteristics enable the camel to endure harsh desert conditions. It can completely close its nostrils, thus protecting it from the stinging effects of sandstorms. Its eyes are shielded from sand and sun by overhanging lids and long lashes, and its broad, padded feet keep it from sinking into the soft sand. No other animal is better equipped for life in the desert than the camel.

GO

1. **What is the main idea expressed in this story?**

   Ⓐ The dromedary is the ideal animal for desert life.

   Ⓑ The camel's hump serves as its food reservoir.

   Ⓒ The dromedary is called the "ship of the desert."

   Ⓓ Camels do not store water in their humps.

2. **Which characteristic does not help the camel to survive in the desert?**

   Ⓕ A camel can drink up to 53 gallons of water in one day.

   Ⓖ A camel can close its nostrils.

   Ⓗ A camel sweats very little.

   Ⓙ A camel is indispensable to desert travel.

3. **What cannot be concluded from reading this passage?**

   Ⓐ A camel can survive a long time without eating.

   Ⓑ A dromedary camel is easier to ride than a Bactrian camel.

   Ⓒ Camels have many features that equip them for cold weather.

   Ⓓ both B and C

4. **Which of these statements is a fact?**

   Ⓕ Nomads prefer camels to all other pack animals.

   Ⓖ The Bactrian camel is the best camel for desert travel.

   Ⓗ A camel's broad, padded feet protect it from sinking in soft sand.

   Ⓙ Camels enjoy hot weather.

5. **Which additional detail would support the title of this story?**

   Ⓐ Nomads use camel's hair to weave cloth to make tents.

   Ⓑ Camels are strong animals capable of carrying loads up to a thousand pounds.

   Ⓒ Camel's milk and meat are often part of the nomad's diet.

   Ⓓ Camels can be stubborn.

6. **For what purpose would you read this passage?**

   Ⓕ to be entertained

   Ⓖ to be informed

   Ⓗ to be persuaded

   Ⓙ to purchase a product

7. **How can you tell when a dromedary needs food?**

   Ⓐ Its eyelids overhang the eyes.

   Ⓑ Its hump becomes smaller.

   Ⓒ It drinks more water.

   Ⓓ Its nostrils completely close.

8. **Which of these statements is an opinion?**

   Ⓕ The dromedary transports people in the Sahara Desert.

   Ⓖ The hump on the dromedary's back serves as its food reserve.

   Ⓗ The dromedary's eyelids protect its eyes from the sand.

   Ⓙ The dromedary is the most interesting desert animal.

English Language Arts

| 1.0 |

Applying Appropriate Reading Strategies
Reading and Comprehension

DIRECTIONS: Read the passages and then answer the questions on the next page.

A

Rose, harsh rose,
marred and with stint of petals,
meager flower thin, sparse of leaf,
more precious
than a wet rose
single on a stem—
you are caught in the drift.

B

   Born in 1888, Huddie Ledbetter, nicknamed "Leadbelly," was a blues guitarist who inspired generations of musicians. For much of his life, he wandered from place to place, playing anywhere he could. In 1934, he was discovered by John and Alan Lomax, who helped him find a larger audience for his music. Soon, he was playing in colleges, clubs, and music halls. He was featured on radio and television shows. Leadbelly died in 1949, but his music lives on. Musicians in every style credit him with laying the foundation for today's popular music.

C

   Frivolous lawsuits have repeatedly been in the news. The family of Giovanni A. Almovodar, New Jersey prison inmate, filed a lawsuit against the Camden County Jail. The inmate was 18 and awaiting trial on a murder charge. He died when he fell on his head during an escape attempt. The family charged that the jailers did not maintain a reasonably safe facility.

D

   The grandmother didn't want to go to Florida. She wanted to visit some of her connections in east Tennessee and she was seizing at every chance to change Bailey's mind. Bailey was the son she lived with, her only boy. He was sitting on the edge of his chair at the table, bent over the orange sports section of the *Journal*. "Now look here, Bailey," she said, "see here, read this," and she stood with one hand on her thin hip and the other rattling the newspaper at his bald head.

E

   What triggers lightning? One theory states that a bigger bit of ice slams into a smaller bit of ice, leaving behind a positive or negative charge. The larger the bit of ice and the faster it is going, the bigger the charge it leaves behind. When enough of these charges collect, lightning occurs.

F

COOK: Short-order cook needed at Flynn's Diner. Shift: 12 midnight to 8 A.M. Must have reliable transportation and references. Good pay and benefits. Two free meals daily. Apply in person at Flynn's Diner, 2000 Wharf Street, near the harbor.

Sources: Selection A—from "Sea Rose," by H. D. [Hilda Doolittle], from *The Norton Anthology of Poetry, Revised Edition*, New York: Norton, 1975, p. 1009. Selection D— from "A Good Man Is Hard to Find," by Flannery O'Connor, from *Anthology of American Literature, Volume 2: Realism to the Present*, New York: Macmillan, 1980, pp. 1739–1750.

GO

1. **Which of the following passages are nonfiction?**

    (A)   passage B

    (B)   passage C

    (C)   passage E

    (D)   all of the above

2. **Which passage requires you to pay particular attention to figurative language?**

    (F)   passage A

    (G)   passage B

    (H)   passage E

    (J)   passage F

3. **Which passage would you be more likely to read with an eye to literal truth?**

    (A)   passage A

    (B)   passage C

    (C)   passage D

    (D)   passage F

4. **Which passage could you more easily illustrate on a time line?**

    (F)   passage A

    (G)   passage B

    (H)   passage E

    (J)   passage F

5. **Which passage requires you to pay particular attention to a sequence of events?**

    (A)   passage A

    (B)   passage C

    (C)   passage D

    (D)   passage E

6. **Which passage would you read to be entertained?**

    (F)   passage B

    (G)   passage C

    (H)   passage D

    (J)   passage E

7. **Which passage would you read to be informed?**

    (A)   passage B

    (B)   passage C

    (C)   passage E

    (D)   all of the above

8. **Which passage is biographical?**

    (F)   passage B

    (G)   passage C

    (H)   passage D

    (J)   passage F

9. **Which passage would you find in a local newspaper?**

    (A)   passage A

    (B)   passage C

    (C)   passage E

    (D)   passage F

STOP

Name _____ Date _____

Identifying Genres
Reading and Comprehension

DIRECTIONS: Based on the passages below, identify the genre of literature of each.

 Clue Genre is a type, or category, of literature. Some examples of genre include fiction, nonfiction, biographies, poetry, plays, and fables.

1. **Act IV**

   Timothy enters his apartment and finds the furniture overturned and things thrown from the drawers. He picks up the telephone and dials 9-1-1.

   TIMOTHY: (fearfully) Yes, I need to report a break-in! (pause) No, I haven't searched the entire apartment. (pause) Do you really think they could still be here?!

   _____

2. **The children awoke to a happy sight.**

   While they were sleeping, the world had turned white.

   Their mother peered into their room and said, "No school today. Go back to bed!"

   _____

3. **Raccoon sat on the beach eating his potato. Before each bite, he dipped the potato into the water. Monkey watched him from his perch in the tree and wondered about this curious habit.**

   _____

4. **The Himalayas are sometimes called the tallest mountains on Earth. The truth is that several underwater ranges are even higher.**

   A passage like this would most likely be found in a book of _____ .

   (A) fables

   (B) facts

   (C) tall tales

   (D) adventure stories

DIRECTIONS: Based on the titles below, identify the genre of literature of each.

5. *King Arthur and the Blazing Sword*

   (F) novel

   (G) play

   (H) legend

   (J) folktale

6. *Adventure to Venus*

   (A) novel

   (B) poetry

   (C) legend

   (D) folktale

7. "Ode to an Owl, the Wisest of Fowl"

   (F) play

   (G) legend

   (H) novel

   (J) poetry

8. *How Zebra Got His Stripes*

   (A) biography

   (B) folktale

   (C) poetry

   (D) novel

9. *Abraham Lincoln: His Life Story*

   (F) legend

   (G) poem

   (H) novel

   (J) biography

GO

DIRECTIONS: The following list tells you about four genres. Read each story below and then write the genre of each on the line that follows.

Science Fiction: a make-believe story based on scientific possibilities. Science fiction is also called fantasy, but it can include scientific facts.

Myth: a make-believe story that explains how something came to be. Myths often describe how the world was created.

Nonfiction: factual information. Nonfiction stories are true.

Realistic Fiction: a make-believe story that could actually happen. These stories aren't true, but it's easy to believe they are.

Juniper trees grow in Arizona. Tiny fairies live in their trunks. During the full moon, the fairies come out and dance at night. While dancing, they place blue berries on each tree for decoration. That's how the juniper gets its berries.

10. _____

"It's a bird!" Tim shouted. "It's a plane!" Connie said. But it was a spaceship! It landed next to a juniper tree. Little green men got off the spaceship. They clipped off several branches of the tree. "They're collecting tree samples to study on Mars," Connie whispered. They watched, amazed, as the spaceship disappeared into the sky.

11. _____

Jason and Patrick went for a hike. Because they were in the high desert, they carried water with them. When they got tired, the two boys sat in the shade of a juniper tree to rest and drink their water. That's when the rattlesnake appeared. "Don't move!" Patrick said to Jason. The boys sat still until the snake moved away. "What an adventure!" Jason said as the two boys returned home.

12. _____

Juniper trees are small, gnarly trees that grow in many parts of the world. Members of the evergreen family, they remain green year round. Juniper trees can be easily identified by their tiny blue or red berries. There are 13 different kinds of juniper trees in the United States. One kind of juniper tree is called the *alligator juniper* because its bark looks similar to the skin of an alligator. It grows in the Southwest.

13. _____

English Language Arts

3.0

Identifying
Unknown Words
Reading and Comprehension

DIRECTIONS: Read each item. Choose the correct meaning for each underlined word.

1. The <u>passage</u> appeared in the magazine.
    - (A) exit
    - (B) crossing
    - (C) journey
    - (D) quotation

2. I <u>introduced</u> my dad to my teacher.
    - (F) proposed
    - (G) familiarized
    - (H) submitted
    - (J) suggested

3. The boat pulled up to the <u>landing</u>.
    - (A) touching down
    - (B) a dock
    - (C) the level part of a staircase
    - (D) taking off

4. The horses were <u>sheltered</u> in the barn.
    - (F) housed
    - (G) shielded
    - (H) concealed
    - (J) exposed

5. Karyn <u>registered</u> for the computer class.
    - (A) listed
    - (B) enlisted
    - (C) enrolled
    - (D) noticed

6. The poet led a <u>colorful</u> life.
    - (F) bright
    - (G) brilliant
    - (H) distinctive or unique
    - (J) multicolored

7. The deer was hidden in a <u>stand</u> of trees.
    - (A) a small retail business
    - (B) a raised platform
    - (C) holding a position
    - (D) a group of plants

8. Facts about antelopes were found in this <u>obscure</u> book.
    - (F) hide
    - (G) little-known
    - (H) baffling
    - (J) mysterious

9. The company <u>recalled</u> the cars because of safety concerns.
    - (A) repealed
    - (B) remembered
    - (C) reinstated
    - (D) summoned

STOP

English Language Arts

Using Context Clues
Reading and Comprehension

DIRECTIONS: Read the paragraph. Choose the word that fits best in each numbered blank.

Clue   If you aren't sure which answer is correct, substitute each answer in the blank.

> People who travel or cross the Amazon and Orinoco rivers of South America are careful never to ____**(1)**____ a foot or hand from the side of their boat. Just below the surface of these mighty waters ____**(2)**____ a small fish feared throughout the ____**(3)**____. That fish is the flesh-eating piranha. It has a nasty ____**(4)**____ and an even nastier ____**(5)**____. Although smaller fish make up most of its diet, the piranha will ____**(6)**____ both human beings and other animals.

1.
- (A) lift
- (B) dangle
- (C) withdraw
- (D) brush

2.
- (F) lurks
- (G) nests
- (H) plays
- (J) boasts

3.
- (A) universe
- (B) town
- (C) continent
- (D) village

4.
- (F) habit
- (G) friend
- (H) flavor
- (J) disposition

5.
- (A) smile
- (B) brother
- (C) appetite
- (D) memory

6.
- (F) befriend
- (G) bully
- (H) attack
- (J) analyze

STOP

English Language Arts

1.0–3.0

For pages 9–16

DIRECTIONS: Read the passage below to answer questions 1–4.

Daedalus

According to a Greek myth, Daedalus was a builder who had a son named Icarus. Daedalus designed the labyrinth, a _____ of complicated passages that is very difficult to escape. Minos, the king of the island Crete, used the labyrinth to hide a monster, called *Minotaur,* who was half man and half bull.

Daedalus did something to anger Minos, and the king made Daedalus and Icarus prisoners in the labyrinth. One day, Daedalus got an idea as he was watching birds fly. He asked Icarus to gather up all the bird feathers he could find. Then, using the feathers and some wax, Daedalus created two large pairs of wings. Soon, he and Icarus were on their way over the walls of the labyrinth.

1. **Which of the following was most likely the source of Daedalus's ideas for inventions?**

    (A) Greek architecture

    (B) the world of nature

    (C) books and drawings

    (D) the suggestions of King Minos

2. **This passage is which genre of literature?**

    (F) biography

    (G) myth

    (H) nonfiction

    (J) poetry

3. **Which of the following words fits best in the blank in the passage?**

    (A) world

    (B) space

    (C) maze

    (D) sea

4. **For what purpose would you read this passage?**

    (F) to be entertained

    (G) to be informed

    (H) to be persuaded

    (J) all of the above

DIRECTIONS: Choose the answer that means the same or about the same as the underlined word.

5. **The twins mustered their courage.**

    (A) lost

    (B) faked

    (C) proclaimed

    (D) gathered

6. **A diminutive woman**

    (F) tiny

    (G) industrious

    (H) slow

    (J) energetic

DIRECTIONS: Read the passage below and then answer question 7.

As she walked along the sandy shore with delight at nature's wonders, she did see starfish, whitecaps, conch shells, and more. She knew that she would never fly free like the tissue-paper seagulls above or swim with the dolphins she did love.

7. **What type of fiction is the passage above?**

    (A) novel

    (B) poem

    (C) play

    (D) folktale

STOP

English Language Arts

4.0

Using Nouns
Writing

DIRECTIONS: The nouns in the sentences below are underlined. Write **C** above each common noun. Write **P** above each proper noun.

> **Examples:**
>
> A common noun names any person, place, or thing. For example: *My aunt visited the museum.*
>
> A proper noun names a particular person, place, or thing. Proper nouns are capitalized. For example: *Aunt Laura visited the Smithsonian Institution.*

1. My friend, Jim, likes to explore our city.

2. Last week, Jim visited the Natural History Museum.

3. Uncle Jasper took him to see the Dallas Museum of Art.

4. Jim enjoyed seeing the paintings at the museum.

5. Next, Jim wants to go to the Texas State Fair.

6. The fair is held at Fair Park every October.

DIRECTIONS: Write a proper noun for each common noun below. Then, write a sentence for each proper noun. The first one is done for you.

7. street   Main Street

   We watched the parade go down Main Street.

8. store   _____

   _____

9. club   _____

10. relative   _____

   _____

11. school   _____

   _____

12. company   _____

   _____

DIRECTIONS: Write a paragraph about a time when you and a relative visited a special place. Then, circle all the nouns in your paragraph and tell whether they are common nouns or proper nouns.

_____

_____

_____

_____

_____

_____

_____

_____

_____

STOP

English Language Arts

4.0 # Using Pronouns and Verbs
Writing

DIRECTIONS: Correct each underlined verb below.

Clue

Pronouns must agree with the verbs to which they refer. When verbs are used in the present tense, the pronoun *she, he,* or *it* makes the verb change a bit. *She (he, it)* **sees** *koalas when she visits Australia. See* has an **s** added to it. But in *We (you, they) see koalas when we visit Australia, see* has no **s** at the end.

The verb *to have* becomes *has* or *have* depending on the pronoun. *We* **have** *to see the koala,* not *We* **has** *to see the koala.* The verb *to be* uses *is* and *are* in the present tense. *We* **are** *going to see koalas,* not *We* **is** *going to see koalas.*

1. **They has an important place in the island continent of Australia.** _____

2. **They attracts millions of visitors to Australia.** _____

3. **They is often called koala bears, but they is marsupials.** _____ _____

4. **We protects this precious symbol of their country.** _____

5. **They has sharp, curved claws to protect themselves.** _____

6. **They climbs trees, often with their babies on their backs.** _____

7. **They eats only the leaves of eucalyptus trees.** _____

8. **We is going to have koalas at our zoo.** _____

9. **Their habitat are being destroyed for housing developments.** _____

10. **Killing koalas have been prohibited by law.** _____

DIRECTIONS: Circle the correct verbs and draw a line through the incorrect ones. Write the correct verbs above those that are incorrect.

"We is going to have a good vacation this year, or I'll eat a bug," says Dad. We starts laughing because he say that every year. Every year, something go wrong. So, we starts out for Lucky Fool Camp. The name are enough for my brother and me to know that this are going to be another weird vacation. On the way, Dad get us lost. My brother know how to get to the camp. He have a great sense of direction. We finally gets there, and there's a big sign that says, "Sorry, we is closed due to mosquito infestation." That mean the place are swarming with mosquitoes. In case we doesn't believe, one bite me right away. What now? Dad look so disappointed until Mom say, "I knew this would happen so I've been saving money all year. Here is four plane tickets to Disney World!" Dad give each of us a big hug. We have our first great vacation!

STOP

English Language Arts

4.0

Subject and Verb Agreement

Writing

> **Examples:**
>
> - A singular subject must have a singular verb as a partner. A plural subject must have a plural verb as a partner. Example: *People are living longer in many countries. People* is a plural subject, so the plural verb *are* is used with it.
> - If two singular words appear together as compound subjects, the verb will be plural. Example: *Hank and Sandy think they passed the test,* not *Hank and Sandy thinks they passed the test.*
> - If a compound subject is joined with *either—or, neither—nor,* the verb must agree with the subject that is closer to the verb. Example: *Neither my brother nor I think we look alike. Either my dog or my cats are making noise outside.*
> - Words such as *everyone, anyone, no one, somebody, someone, something* are called **singular indefinite pronouns.** They always require a singular verb. Example: *Everyone who comes to my party is bringing a gift,* not *Everyone who comes to my party are bringing a gift.*

DIRECTIONS: Write the correct verb form to match each subject in the story below.

Cormorants _____ (is, are) birds that

help people. In some countries, this type of bird

_____ (is, are) used to help catch fish!

Cormorants _____ (fly, flies) around fishing

grounds. Fishermen watching them know where the

fish _____ (is, are). Some fishermen _____

(catch, catches) cormorants. They _____

(tie, ties) long cords to the birds, then _____

(take, takes) them out on their boats. When the birds

_____ (dive, dives) under the water to catch fish,

the fishermen _____ (keep, keeps) them from

making off with the fish. Cormorants _____

(is, are) related to pelicans. Most cormorants

_____ (perch, perches) in trees, on rocks, and

on the edges of cliffs. They _____ (has, have)

webbed feet.

DIRECTIONS: Circle the correct verb in each sentence.

1. **Those toys (is, are) loved by most children.**

2. **There (is, are) two kids who missed the bus.**

3. **Neither my cat nor my dogs (like, likes) to eat pet food.**

4. **There (is, are) no reasons for you to miss school today.**

5. **Facts (is, are) facts, and you can't deny them.**

6. **Many movie monsters (is, are) truly scary.**

7. **Either you or your sister (is, are) going to clean that room.**

8. **Five tomatoes (is, are) growing on the vine.**

English Language Arts

4.0

Simple and
Compound Sentences
Writing

DIRECTIONS: Write *simple* on the lines after the simple sentences and *compound* on the lines after the compound sentences.

1. **It was a beautiful day, and I was ready for adventure.**

   _____

2. **I saw my friend Marcy and invited her to come with me.**

   _____

3. **She strapped on her skates, and she joined me.**

   _____

4. **Marcy and I enjoyed our trip to the park.**

   _____

5. **We reached the park and took a rest.**

   _____

6. **Marcy is new to skating, but I'm not.**

   _____

DIRECTIONS: Choose the answer that best combines the sentences.

7. **Gordon is going to the store.**
   Samantha is going with him.

   (A) Gordon is going to the store and so is Samantha.

   (B) Gordon and Samantha are going to the store.

   (C) To the store, Gordon and Samantha are going.

   (D) Gordon and Samantha to the store are going.

8. **Please go to the refrigerator.**
   I would like you to get a soda for me.

   (F) Please go to the refrigerator to get me a soda.

   (G) Please go to the refrigerator to get me a soda, because I want one.

   (H) For me, please go to the refrigerator to get a soda.

   (J) I would like for you to please go to the refrigerator to get a soda for me.

9. **Ms. Lightfoot loves dancing.**
   She goes to the dance studio every day.
   She goes at eight o'clock.

   (A) Ms. Lightfoot loves dancing, and she goes to the dance studio every day at eight o'clock.

   (B) Ms. Lightfoot goes to the dance studio every day at eight o'clock, because she loves dancing.

   (C) Ms. Lightfoot loves dancing every day at the studio at eight o'clock.

   (D) Every day, Ms. Lightfoot loves going to the dance studio to dance at eight o'clock.

STOP

English Language Arts

5.0

Writing with a Focus
Writing

DIRECTIONS: Sixth graders wrote the following letters as part of a class project. Read the letter in each of the boxes below. Then, answer the questions.

A   Your store is the best grocery store in Orchard Grove. My parents buy all their groceries at your store. Our class is trying to raise money for a class trip. We would like to hold a car wash in your parking lot on Saturday, because we would get lots of business on that day.

B   We have 25 students in our class. Our teacher's name is Mr. Wordsworth. He is a great teacher. He said I should write to ask if we could hold a car wash in your parking lot on Saturday. He thought you would say yes.

C   The students in our class are raising money for our class trip. We would like your permission to hold a car wash in your parking lot on Saturday from 9:00 A.M. to 3:00 P.M. We promise to clean up when we are finished. We appreciate your consideration of this matter.

D   The students in our class think the best place to have a car wash would be in your parking lot. We think we could raise lots of money there. We need money to go on a class trip, since the school will not pay our way. Saturday from 9:00 A.M. to 3:00 P.M. would be a great time for us.

1. **What task does the class have?**
   - (A) to raise money for a class trip
   - (B) to clean their parents' cars
   - (C) to bring more cars to the parking lot
   - (D) to have something to do on a Saturday morning

2. **To whom are the students writing the letter?**
   - (F) to their teacher
   - (G) to their parents
   - (H) to their principal
   - (J) to the owner of the parking lot

3. **Which letter would be most appropriate in asking permission to use the parking lot for a car wash?**
   - (A) Letter A
   - (B) Letter B
   - (C) Letter C
   - (D) Letter D

4. **What point of view do the letters use?**
   - (F) first person
   - (G) second person
   - (H) third person
   - (J) first and third person

STOP

English Language Arts

Using Appropriate Content
Writing

DIRECTIONS: Read this story about Amelia Earhart and then answer the questions that follow.

(1) <u>The weather was bad</u> over the mid-Atlantic Ocean. (2) The small plane's engine sputtered. (3) The slim, young woman at the controls knew she was too far out to turn back. (4) Carefully, she coaxed the plane ahead through the storm.

(5) When dawn came, the engine was failing seriously. (6) Just ahead lay the Irish coast. (7) As the engine gasped its last breath, the woman brought her plane down in a cow pasture. (8) An astonished farmer raced over as the young woman climbed out of the airplane. (9) "I'm from America," she said. (10) "My name is Amelia Earhart." (11) The farmer was angry that she had ruined part of his field. (12) She had even set a new speed record: thirteen hours and thirty minutes!

(13) They didn't think a woman was strong enough to keep going through the long night. (14) However, Earhart had strength and courage to spare. (15) She had already made parachute jumps and had explored the ocean floor in a diver's suit. (16) Now, overnight, she had become famous.

1. Which sentence could be added after sentence 10?

(A) The farmer thought she was an alien from outer space.

(B) She had become the first woman to fly over the Atlantic Ocean alone.

(C) She had become the first woman to safely land in a pasture.

(D) She added, "Do you know where I might get something good to eat?"

2. Which sentence could begin the third paragraph?

(F) Many people had told Amelia not to make this flight.

(G) Amelia wanted to give up.

(H) Amelia was a weak woman.

(J) Amelia loved to set world records.

3. Which group of words would be more colorful than the underlined words in sentence 1?

(A) There was lightning

(B) Lightning ripped through the blackness

(C) It was cold and wet

(D) The weather was stormy

4. Which sentence does not belong in the story?

(F) Sentence 2

(G) Sentence 6

(H) Sentence 11

(J) Sentence 16

STOP

English Language Arts

5.0

Identifying Point of View
Writing

DIRECTIONS: Below are ten short paragraphs. In each blank, write **1** for first person, **2** for second person, or **3** for third person to identify the point of view of each.

Example:

_____ Your heart is thumping in your chest as the car slowly makes its way to the top of the hill. You risk looking down just as the roller coaster reaches the very top and begins its mad drop.

Answer: 2

1. _____ It's true, you know? You always loved cats more than people. When you first saw . . . what was that cat's name? Oh, yes, Bernard! When your dad brought Bernard home from the shelter, you looked like you had gone to heaven and seen an angel.

2. _____ A domestic turkey is not a wise bird. A dog, fox, or weasel that finds its way into a turkey coop merely waits for some lamebrained and curious turkey to waddle over for a visit. The predator has a cooperative victim!

3. _____ I don't think I can stand it any longer. I've got to tell Mom how much I dislike her asparagus custard pie. But how do I do it without hurting her feelings?

4. _____ That stubborn bachelor Patches McCloud had better get out of his termite-infested apartment before the walls come tumbling in on him! No one need warn him again!

5. _____ When you were born, the sun smiled down upon the earth. The moon glowed. The creatures of the night forest whispered that you, a princess, had been born to our people.

6. _____ What? You—become an army sharpshooter? Why, you couldn't hit the broad side of a barn if you were leaning against it!

7. _____ She carried a large basket of laundry on her head. She had done chores like this since she was a tiny child. But this time, things were different. Mikela was working at a real job now. Wouldn't her mother be proud!

8. _____ Oh, it was so dark! We will never know what caused the sudden blackout at the ball game. We hope the game will be rescheduled.

9. _____ The song "Yankee Doodle" was used by British soldiers to mock the colonials who opposed them. But the colonists were smart enough to realize that if they embraced the mockery, it would take the sting out of it. So, the song became their anthem.

10. _____ It's backbreaking work. All day long, we are bent over at the waist as we carefully replant our rice in the flooded paddy. But our feet tingle in the cool, rich, oozing mud.

STOP

Name _____   Date _____

English Language Arts

Spelling and Capitalization
Writing

DIRECTIONS: Fill in the blank with the word that best fits each sentence.

1. No one wanted to _____ (by, buy) the book with the wrinkled cover.

2. The cost of the newspaper has increased to seventy-five _____ (cents, sense).

3. Jamal, the social studies report is _____ (do, dew, due) tomorrow!

4. Call me when _____ (it's, its) my turn to use the computer.

5. We can rest when _____ (their, there, they're) is nothing left to put away.

6. The keys were _____ (here, hear) on the table this morning.

7. We'll get tickets when _____ (their, there, they're) in town next year.

8. Nathan _____ (red, read) a chapter of the book every day after dinner.

9. Show Brendan _____ (where, wear) we keep the extra towels.

DIRECTIONS: Rewrite the following sentences using the correct capitalization.

10. The proclamation of 1763 forbade British subjects to settle beyond the appalachian mountains.

_____

_____

11. During the revolutionary war, fighting occurred from quebec in the north to florida in the south.

_____

_____

_____

12. The Americans were angry about paying the taxes required by the stamp act of 1765.

_____

_____

_____

13. The boston tea party was planned to protest the tea act of 1773.

_____

_____

_____

14. In 1853, the gadsden purchase gave the United States more land.

_____

_____

_____

GO

English Language Arts

6.0

Punctuation
Writing

DIRECTIONS: Fill in the circle for the choice that has a punctuation error. If there are no mistakes, choose "no mistakes."

1. Ⓐ Our teacher Ms. Matthews, is

    Ⓑ treating the class to ice cream sundaes

    Ⓒ at Dairy Delight, my favorite ice cream shop.

    Ⓓ no mistakes

2. Ⓕ "I miss Grandpa," said Casey,

    Ⓖ "Can we see him again soon?"

    Ⓗ She loved her grandpa very much.

    Ⓙ no mistakes

3. Ⓐ 8789 Rachel Dr.

    Ⓑ Aarontown, MI 49543

    Ⓒ May 22 2002.

    Ⓓ no mistakes

4. Ⓕ Dear Melvin

    Ⓖ   I was so pleased to hear you won the

    Ⓗ scholarship to computer camp. Good job!

    Ⓙ no mistakes

5. Ⓐ You will have to show me all you learned?

    Ⓑ Sincerely,

    Ⓒ Margie

    Ⓓ no mistakes

DIRECTIONS: Choose the word or words that fit best in the blank and show the correct punctuation.

6. _____ please remember to wash your hands.

    Ⓕ Brewster

    Ⓖ Brewster:

    Ⓗ Brewster,

    Ⓙ "Brewster"

7. The _____ bite was bigger than its bark.

    Ⓐ dogs

    Ⓑ dog's

    Ⓒ dogs's

    Ⓓ dogs'

8. Charlene needed to bring _____ to the picnic.

    Ⓕ plates, napkins, and cups

    Ⓖ plates napkins and cups

    Ⓗ plates, napkins, and cups,

    Ⓙ plates, napkins and, cups

9. This bus is _____ we'll have to catch the next one.

    Ⓐ full

    Ⓑ full,

    Ⓒ full;

    Ⓓ full:

STOP

English Language Arts

6.0

Using Figurative Language
Writing

DIRECTIONS: For each sentence below, write a more colorful way to express the same idea. Use whatever types of figurative language you want (simile, metaphor, personification, idiom, etc.).

> **Examples:**
>
> - **Personification** assigns human qualities, feelings, or actions to an animal, an object, or an idea. Example: The mother bear cried for her cub.
> - **Similes** use *like* or *as* to compare things that may seem unlike each other. Example: Her smile was as dazzling as the sun.
> - **Metaphors** compare unlike things but without using *like* or *as*. Example: His body was a well-oiled machine.
> - **Idioms** are expressions that mean something different from what they actually say. Example: She kept a chip on her shoulder.

1. The weather was bad over the ocean today.

   _____

   _____

   _____

2. Jana was angry with Martin.

   _____

   _____

   _____

3. Kara was her mother's pride and joy.

   _____

   _____

   _____

4. The knife was sharper than anything Billy had ever felt.

   _____

   _____

   _____

5. These are the best hamburgers I've ever tasted! They're delicious!

   _____

   _____

   _____

6. Alex walked slowly as he carried the heavy suitcase back to the attic.

   _____

   _____

   _____

7. It was a bright, beautiful, sunshiny day.

   _____

   _____

   _____

8. The loud chirping of the crickets woke Keisha from a deep sleep.

   _____

   _____

   _____

STOP

English Language Arts

4.0–6.0

For pages 18–27

Mini-Test 2

Writing

DIRECTIONS: Choose the answer that shows the best capitalization and punctuation.

1. His family is from austin the capital of the state of Texas.

- (A) austin the
- (B) austin, the
- (C) Austin, the
- (D) correct as it is

2. Jennifer loves fish; Tess loathes it.

- (F) fish, Tess
- (G) fish: Tess
- (H) fish. Tess
- (J) correct as it is

3. Grandma will sit next to me and Grandpa will sit by you.

- (A) me, and,
- (B) me and,
- (C) me, and
- (D) correct as it is

DIRECTIONS: Circle the correct word to complete the following sentences.

4. (They're/Their) planning to be here by noon tomorrow.

5. Everything should be in (it's/its) correct place when you are finished.

6. We (is/are) so excited to see you.

7. Somebody (has/have) chosen the red and white streamers.

DIRECTIONS: Use the paragraph below to answer questions 8–10.

(1) *This is a pretty good poem,* she thought to herself. (2) *It's just that . . .* (3) Lois wondered if she had fed her dog before she left for school. (4) Then, her name was called, she stood up, and her knees began to shake. (5) When she turned around and looked at the rest of the class, however, she saw friendly faces.

8. Choose the best first sentence for this paragraph.

- (F) Lois waited for her turn to read her poem in front of the class.
- (G) Lois could hardly wait to go to lunch.
- (H) Lois was looking forward to reading her play.
- (J) Lois loved English class.

9. Which sentence should be left out of this paragraph?

- (A) Sentence 1
- (B) Sentence 2
- (C) Sentence 3
- (D) Sentence 5

10. What point of view is used in this passage?

- (F) first person
- (G) second person
- (H) third person
- (J) first and third person

STOP

Locating Information in Texts
Research

DIRECTIONS: Choose the best answer.

1. **While doing research for a report, Wanda used the book titled *Technology Tomorrow*. Where in the book should Wanda look to learn what information is found in each chapter?**

   A the index

   B the table of contents

   C the title page

   D the introduction

2. **Where in the book should Wanda look to learn when the book was published?**

   F the index

   G the table of contents

   H the copyright page

   J the bibliography

3. **Where in the book should Wanda look to learn what other sources she might be able to use for her report?**

   A the index

   B the table of contents

   C the title page

   D the bibliography

4. **Because Wanda has used other sources to write her report, she should _____ .**

   F explain in her introduction that she has used other sources

   G make photocopies of her sources and attach them to her report

   H acknowledge her sources in citations and a bibliography

   J ignore the sources because she is only writing a report for school

---

Index

Engines
fuel, 32–36
types of, 30–38

History
in Africa, 18–22
in Asia, 20–24
in Europe, 2–10
in North America, 8–18
in South America, 16–18
legends and stories, 72–78

Tracks
laying, 26–32
types, 28–33, 93–95

Workers
job classifications, 80–85
unions, 4–8

---

5. **The index above appears in a book about trains. Which pages would probably tell about a Ghost Train some people say they have seen?**

   A 72–78

   B 32–36

   C 80–85

   D 28–33

6. **Which pages would give you information on trains that ran between France and Germany during the 1930s?**

   F 4–8

   G 18–22

   H 2–10

   J 16–18

STOP

English Language Arts

8.0

Using Technological Resources
Research

DIRECTIONS: Read the passage. Then, answer the questions on the next page.

Niagara Falls

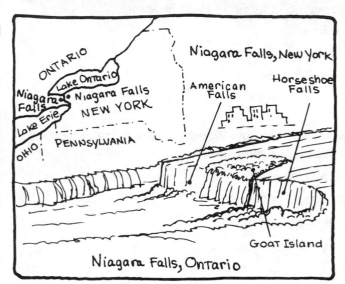

Niagara Falls, Ontario

Niagara Falls is one of the most spectacular natural wonders of the world. Part of the Falls is in Ontario, Canada, and part is in New York State.

The Falls are supplied by the Niagara River, which connects Lake Ontario and Lake Erie. The Niagara Falls are located midway in the river. They pour 500,000 tons of water a minute into a deep gorge.

Scientists believe that Niagara Falls was formed after the last ice sheet from the Ice Age withdrew from the area. The surface of the land was changed by the ice. This caused waterways and streams to form new paths. The result was an overflow of Lake Erie, which produced Niagara Falls. Scientists believe that the Falls are approximately 20,000 years old.

The Falls are formed over an outer layer of hard dolomitic limestone. This covers a softer layer of shale. The shale is more easily worn away, which causes the harder limestone to form an overhanging edge. This allows the Falls to drop straight down at a sharp angle, which produces a spectacular sight.

Over the years, the outer layer has broken off at times. This is causing the Falls to gradually move back up the river. This erosion is happening to the American Falls at the rate of three to seven inches a year. But the edge of the Horseshoe Falls is being worn back at the rate of approximately three feet a year.

Over the years, Niagara Falls has been a spectacular attraction for sightseers. Observation towers and a special area, Cave of the Winds, behind the Falls, have allowed remarkable views. At night, the Falls are flooded with lights. A steamer, called *Maid of the Mist,* takes visitors for a ride around the base of the Falls.

Niagara Falls has also irresistibly drawn daredevils who have wanted to test their courage. One such man, Charles Blondin, crossed the Falls on a tightrope in 1859. Four days later, he crossed again, only this time with a blindfold. A month later, he crossed for the third time carrying a man on his shoulders. And as if that weren't daring enough, he returned to cross the Falls once again—on stilts!

GO

Clue If you do not have access to the Internet, use library resources to answer the questions.

1. **Use an online dictionary to find definitions to at least three terms in the passage. Write each word and its definition in the space below. (Hint: Both *www.dictionary.com* and *www.m-w.com/home.htm* are good online dictionaries.)**

   Term: _____

   Definition: _____

   _____

   _____

   Term: _____

   Definition: _____

   _____

   _____

   Term: _____

   Definition: _____

   _____

   _____

2. **Use an online search engine to locate pictures of Niagara Falls. Did the pictures help you understand the passage better? Explain your answer.**

   _____

   _____

   _____

   _____

3. **Use the Internet resource of your choice to find the nationality and real name of Charles Blondin, who walked across the Falls on a tightrope in 1859. Briefly report your findings.**

   _____

   _____

   _____

   _____

STOP

English Language Arts

7.0–8.0

For pages 29–31

Mini-Test 3

Research

DIRECTIONS: Use the index below to answer questions 1 and 2.

Index

aspirin, 41, 170

brain, 171

calcium, 53, 193

eardrums, 179

food allergies, 39, 167

insect bites, 48, 183

lips, 179

1. **On which page would you find information about why some people cannot eat nuts?**

    (A)   page 48

    (B)   page 171

    (C)   page 193

    (D)   page 39

2. **On which page might fleas, fire ants, and wasps be mentioned?**

    (F)   page 39

    (G)   page 48

    (H)   page 53

    (J)   page 179

DIRECTIONS: Choose the best answer.

3. **Kim is about to begin reading a book titled *Let Liberty Ring*. Where in the book should Kim look to find out when the book was published?**

    (A)   the table of contents

    (B)   the copyright page

    (C)   the introduction

    (D)   the index

4. **Where would you find information about the sources an author used to write a book?**

    (F)   title page

    (G)   index

    (H)   bibliography

    (J)   table of contents

5. **If you wanted to find a definition for the word *metamorphosis,* which reference would you use?**

    (A)   a dictionary

    (B)   an encyclopedia

    (C)   an atlas

    (D)   a thesaurus

DIRECTIONS: Read the paragraph below. Then, answer the question that follows.

One of the nicest things about summer evenings is being able to watch fireflies or try to catch them. Did you ever wonder why fireflies light up? Some scientists think the lights are used to scare away birds that might eat the fireflies. Others think the fireflies use their lights to say "Hello" to their future mates.

6. **What resources would you use to find out more information about fireflies and why they light up?**

    _____

    _____

    _____

    _____

    _____

    _____

    _____

STOP

Name _____ Date _____

English Language Arts

9.0

Comparing Works from Different Times and Places
Cultural and Social Language Use

DIRECTIONS: Visit the library or go online to find information about the works listed in the table below. For each work, identify the genre and the culture where it originated. Then, pick one of the works, find a copy online or at the library, and read it. Compare it to something else you've recently read.

	Genre	Culture
Beowulf		
Anansie tales		
The Twenty-Two Goblins		
"The Two Frogs"		
The Nose		
A Modest Proposal		
"The Animals Sick of the Plague"		
"Ode on a Grecian Urn"		

Title of historical work:

_____

_____

_____

Title of recently read work:

_____

_____

_____

What are some basic similarities and differences in the themes, plot, and language between the two works?

_____

_____

_____

_____

_____

_____

_____

_____

STOP

English Language Arts

11.0

Writing
About Community
Cultural and Social Language Use

DIRECTIONS: Write three short paragraphs about ways that you could volunteer in your community. Structure your composition as follows.

Paragraph 1: Choose at least three organizations for which you would be interested in doing volunteer work. Describe them.

Paragraph 2: Give reasons why you would be interested in volunteering for these organizations.

Paragraph 3: Conclude by explaining what contributions you personally could make as a volunteer for these organizations.

_____

_____

_____

_____

_____

_____

_____

_____

_____

_____

_____

_____

_____

_____

_____

_____

_____

_____

_____

_____

STOP

English Language Arts

| 12.0 |

Writing
to Communicate
Cultural and Social Language Use

DIRECTIONS: Write a composition responding to the following question: Do you think there is too much violence on TV, in the movies, and in video games? Answer the following questions to organize your information.

1. **What do you think are the effects of showing violence on TV, in the movies, and in video games?**

   _____

   _____

   _____

   _____

   _____

   _____

2. **Find graphs, charts, or other visuals that give you information about the topic. What information do they provide? Include the graphs and charts with your composition.**

   _____

   _____

   _____

   _____

   _____

   _____

3. **What sources did you use to find more information on the topic?**

   _____

   _____

   _____

   _____

   _____

   _____

4. **What are possible solutions to the problem?**

   _____

   _____

   _____

   _____

   _____

   _____

DIRECTIONS: Now, on a separate sheet of paper, write your composition. Remember to clearly state your purpose for writing, develop your topic with supporting details, and conclude with a detailed summary.

STOP

English Language Arts
| 9.0–12.0 |

For pages 33–35

Mini-Test 4

Cultural and Social Language Use

DIRECTIONS: Write three paragraphs about what you think is the biggest problem facing world leaders today. Identify the problem and explain why you think it is the most serious problem. Then, explain what you think world leaders could do to solve the problem.

_____

_____

_____

_____

_____

_____

_____

_____

_____

_____

_____

_____

_____

_____

_____

_____

_____

_____

_____

_____

_____

_____

_____

STOP

How Am I Doing?

Mini-Test 1

Page 17

Number Correct

7 answers correct		**Great Job!** Move on to the section test on page 39.
5–6 answers correct		**You're almost there!** But you still need a little practice. Review practice pages 9–16 before moving on to the section test on page 39.
0–4 answers correct		**Oops!** Time to review what you have learned and try again. Review the practice section on pages 9–16. Then, retake the test on page 17. Now, move on to the section test on page 39.

Mini-Test 2

Page 28

Number Correct

9–10 answers correct		**Awesome!** Move on to the section test on page 39.
6–8 answers correct		**You're almost there!** But you still need a little practice. Review practice pages 18–27 before moving on to the section test on page 39.
0–5 answers correct		**Oops!** Time to review what you have learned and try again. Review the practice section on pages 18–27. Then, retake the test on page 28. Now, move on to the section test on page 39.

Mini-Test 3

Page 32

Number Correct

6 answers correct		**Great Job!** Move on to the section test on page 39.
4–5 answers correct		**You're almost there!** But you still need a little practice. Review practice pages 29–31 before moving on to the section test on page 39.
0–3 answers correct		**Oops!** Time to review what you have learned and try again. Review the practice section on pages 29–31. Then, retake the test on page 32. Now, move on to the section test on page 39.

How Am I Doing?

Mini-Test 4	1 answer correct	**Great Job!** Move on to the section test on page 39.
Page 36 **Number Correct**	0 answers correct	**Oops!** Time to review what you have learned and try again. Review the practice section on pages 33–35. Then, retake the test on page 36. Now, move on to the section test on page 39.

Final English Language Arts Test
for pages 9–35

DIRECTIONS: Read the passage below, and then answer the questions that follow.

Act I, Scene 1

Cheryl enters the room carrying her lunch tray and sits across the table from her friend Heather.
CHERYL: Heather, I need an objective opinion. Tracy says I'm a liar.
HEATHER: *(crunching a carrot)* About what?
CHERYL: It doesn't matter. I'm honest, right?
HEATHER: Honest about what?
CHERYL: *(smiling)* You know, trustworthy, direct, truthful.
HEATHER: Well . . . *(hesitating)* Now don't fly off the handle, Cheryl, but what about the time you lied to your folks about your math grade?
CHERYL: Math grades don't count.

1. **This passage is an example of what genre?**
   - (A) short story
   - (B) play
   - (C) poem
   - (D) fable

2. **The phrase *fly off the handle* is _____ .**
   - (F) an idiom
   - (G) a simile
   - (H) alliteration
   - (J) personification

DIRECTIONS: Read the paragraph below and then answer the questions that follow.

An urban habitat is home to many animals. A rural habitat is also home to a variety of animals. Birds, such as pigeons and starlings, nest on tall buildings. Mice and rats build their nests in or near buildings. Squirrels, rabbits, and opossums make their homes in the wide-open spaces of city parks. Timid animals like foxes and raccoons search for food in neighborhood garbage cans at night. Perhaps the favorite city animals, though, are the ones that live in the homes of people—cats, dogs, and other animal friends we call pets.

3. **What is the main idea of this paragraph?**
   - (A) People should protect city animals.
   - (B) Urban animals cause many problems.
   - (C) Many animals live in the city.
   - (D) People who live in cities should not have pets.

4. **What is the author's purpose for writing this paragraph?**
   - (F) to inform people about animals that live in urban habitats
   - (G) to warn people about urban animals
   - (H) to persuade city officials about the need to protect animals
   - (J) to entertain people with stories about urban animals

5. **Which sentence does not belong in this paragraph?**
   - (A) Birds, such as pigeons and starlings, nest on tall buildings.
   - (B) An urban habitat is home to many animals.
   - (C) A rural habitat is also home to a variety of animals.
   - (D) Mice and rats build their nests in or near buildings.

6. **What point of view is used in this paragraph?**
   - (F) first person
   - (G) second person
   - (H) third person
   - (J) first and third person

GO

DIRECTIONS: Choose the best answer.

7. **Which of the following is a simile?**

   (A) The bread was not as soft as it should have been.

   (B) The bread was left out and became stale.

   (C) The bread was as hard as a rock.

   (D) The bread was delicious with strawberry jam.

8. **Which of the following is a metaphor?**

   (F) His harsh words were difficult for Dana to take.

   (G) His words were hammers, pounding at Dana.

   (H) Dana was upset by his harsh words.

   (J) His harsh words made Dana's head pound.

DIRECTIONS: For numbers 9–11, choose the correct verb form to match each subject in the sentences.

9. **Many animals _____ in trees.**

   (A) live

   (B) lives

   (C) living

   (D) had live

10. **The animals _____ shy and afraid of people.**

    (F) be

    (G) is

    (H) are

    (J) been

11. **They _____ everyone with their behavior.**

    (A) shock

    (B) is shocking

    (C) shocks

    (D) shocking

DIRECTIONS: Read the passage and then choose the word that best fits each blank.

Laughter is good medicine. Scientists believe that laughter _____(12)_____ the heart and lungs. Laughter burns calories and may help _____(13)_____ blood pressure. It also _____(14)_____ stress and tension. If you are _____(15)_____ about an upcoming test, laughter can help you relax.

12.　(F) damages

    (G) stresses

    (H) weakens

    (J) strengthens

13.　(A) raise

    (B) lower

    (C) eliminate

    (D) elongate

14.　(F) relieves

    (G) increases

    (H) revives

    (J) releases

15.　(A) excited

    (B) enthusiastic

    (C) nervous

    (D) knowledgeable

GO

DIRECTIONS: Decide which punctuation mark is needed in each sentence.

16. "This is fun, answered Lettie.
- (F) ,
- (G) ?
- (H) "
- (J) '

17. Jeff will you please bring in the newspaper?
- (A) ,
- (B) !
- (C) "
- (D) '

18. Youre early today.
- (F) ,
- (G) ?
- (H) "
- (J) '

DIRECTIONS: Choose the answer that best combines the sentences.

19. George left early.
    Carol left early.
    They are going to the band festival.
- (A) George and Carol left early because to the band festival they are going.
- (B) George and Carol left early to go to the band festival.
- (C) George left early and Carol because they are going to the band festival.
- (D) Leaving early, George and Carol are going to the band festival.

DIRECTIONS: Choose the answer that has correct spelling, capitalization, and punctuation.

20. She lives on _____ just two blocks away.
- (F) Fifth street. Its
- (G) Fifth Street, its
- (H) Fifth Street. It's
- (J) fifth street, it's

21. _____ showed them how to floss.
- (A) Their dentist, Dr. Newman,
- (B) They're dentist, Dr. Newman,
- (C) Their Dentist, Dr. Newman,
- (D) Their dentist Dr. Newman

DIRECTIONS: Use the table of contents below to answer questions 22 and 23.

Table of Contents	
Chapter	**Page**
1 The Natural World 3	
2 The Human Body 33	
3 The Home Planet 59	
4 Numbers and Formulas 71	

22. Which of these topics would most likely be found in chapter 3?
- (F) jet engines
- (G) hay fever
- (H) Earth
- (J) lips

23. In which chapter would you probably find information about the liver's function?
- (A) chapter 1
- (B) chapter 2
- (C) chapter 3
- (D) chapter 4

STOP

Final English Language Arts Test

Answer Sheet

1. (A) (B) (C) (D)
2. (F) (G) (H) (J)
3. (A) (B) (C) (D)
4. (F) (G) (H) (J)
5. (A) (B) (C) (D)
6. (F) (G) (H) (J)
7. (A) (B) (C) (D)
8. (F) (G) (H) (J)
9. (A) (B) (C) (D)
10. (F) (G) (H) (J)

11. (A) (B) (C) (D)
12. (F) (G) (H) (J)
13. (A) (B) (C) (D)
14. (F) (G) (H) (J)
15. (A) (B) (C) (D)
16. (F) (G) (H) (J)
17. (A) (B) (C) (D)
18. (F) (G) (H) (J)
19. (A) (B) (C) (D)
20. (F) (G) (H) (J)

21. (A) (B) (C) (D)
22. (F) (G) (H) (J)
23. (A) (B) (C) (D)

Mathematics Standards

Standard 1—Number and Operations *(See pages 44–48.)*
  A. Understand numbers, ways of representing numbers, relationships among numbers, and number systems.
  B. Understand meanings of operations and how they relate to one another.
  C. Compute fluently and make reasonable estimates.

Standard 2—Algebra *(See pages 49–53.)*
  A. Understand patterns, relations, and functions.
  B. Represent and analyze mathematical situations and structures using algebraic symbols.
  C. Use mathematical models to represent and understand quantitative relationships.
  D. Analyze change in various contexts.

Standard 3—Geometry *(See pages 55–60.)*
  A. Analyze characteristics and properties of two- and three-dimensional shapes and develop mathematical arguments about geometric relationships.
  B. Specify locations and describe spatial relationships using coordinate geometry and other representational systems.
  C. Apply transformations and use symmetry to analyze mathematical situations.
  D. Use visualization, spatial reasoning, and geometric modeling to solve problems.

Standard 4—Measurement *(See pages 61–64.)*
  A. Understand measurable attributes of objects and the units, systems, and processes of measurement.
  B. Apply appropriate techniques, tools, and formulas to determine measurement.

Standard 5—Data Analysis and Probability *(See pages 66–69.)*
  A. Formulate questions that can be addressed with data and collect, organize, and display relevant data to answer them.
  B. Select and use appropriate statistical methods to analyze data.
  C. Develop and evaluate inferences and predictions that are based on data.
  D. Understand and apply basic concepts of probability.

Standard 6—Process *(See pages 70–73.)*
  A. Problem Solving
  B. Reasoning and Proof
  C. Communication
  D. Connections
  E. Representation

Prime Factorization
Number and Operations

DIRECTIONS: Find the prime factorization of each composite number. Write the prime factors in numerical order on the leaves of the factor tree. Check your answers by completing the factor tree.

1. **Prime Factorization =** _____

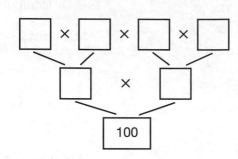

2. **Prime Factorization =** _____

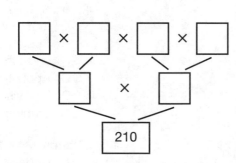

3. **Prime Factorization =** _____

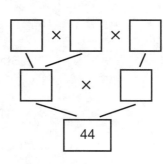

4. **Prime Factorization =** _____

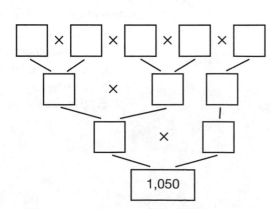

Name _____ Date _____

Mathematics

1.A

Percents, Decimals, and Fractions

Number and Operations

Examples:

Fraction to Decimal:
The fraction bar means divide.

$\frac{3}{5} = 3 \div 5$ $5\overline{)3.0}$ (.6, 30, 0) $\frac{3}{5} = 0.6$

Decimal to Percent:
Move the decimal two places to the right.

$0.08 = 8\%$

$0.73 = 73\%$

Percent to Decimal:
Move the decimal two places to the left.

$42\% = 0.42$

$1.87\% = 0.0187$

Decimal to Fraction:
Write the digits over the appropriate place value and reduce to lowest terms.

$0.35 = \text{thirty-five hundredths} = \frac{35}{100} = \frac{7}{20}$

$0.015 = \text{fifteen thousandths} = \frac{15}{1000} = \frac{3}{200}$

Clue   **Percent** (%) means *per hundred*. It is a ratio that compares a number to 100. It is the number of hundredths.

DIRECTIONS: Write each fraction in decimal form.

1. $\frac{4}{5}$ _____   2. $\frac{3}{8}$ _____   3. $\frac{5}{3}$ _____   4. $\frac{7}{9}$ _____

DIRECTIONS: Change each percent to its decimal form.

5. 39% _____   6. 7% _____   7. 1.8% _____   8. 132% _____   9. 0.05% _____

DIRECTIONS: Change each decimal to its percent form.

10. 0.87 _____   11. 1.20 _____   12. 0.45 _____   13. 0.02 _____   14. 0.342 _____

DIRECTIONS: Change each decimal to a fraction.

15. 0.6 _____   16. 0.42 _____   17. 0.025 _____   18. 0.85 _____   19. 1.92 _____

STOP

Mathematics

1.A

Percentages and Ratios
Number and Operations

DIRECTIONS: Choose the best answer.

1. Pizzazz Pizza Parlor gave the sixth grade class a 25% discount on pizzas they purchased for a party. Each pizza originally cost $12.00. How much did the sixth graders pay per pizza?

   Ⓐ $3.00

   Ⓑ $9.00

   Ⓒ $8.00

   Ⓓ $6.00

2. Twenty-five percent of the workers are on third shift. There are 132 workers in all. How many of them are on third shift?

   Ⓕ 25

   Ⓖ 12

   Ⓗ 33

   Ⓙ 3

3. The enrollment at Franklin School has increased 20% from last year. The enrollment last year was 750. By how many students has the enrollment increased?

   Ⓐ 750

   Ⓑ 900

   Ⓒ 600

   Ⓓ 150

4. Forty percent of the class finished their assignment before lunch. There are 25 students in the class. How many students finished before lunch?

   Ⓕ 40

   Ⓖ 10

   Ⓗ 25

   Ⓙ 12

5. The ratio of two days to four weeks is equivalent to _____ .

   Ⓐ $\frac{1}{2}$

   Ⓑ $\frac{1}{14}$

   Ⓒ $\frac{1}{7}$

   Ⓓ $\frac{1}{16}$

6. The ratio of the scale drawing of Brittany's bedroom to the actual bedroom is 1 inch to 5 feet. If the width of Brittany's bedroom is 15 feet, what should be the width of the bedroom on the scale drawing?

   Ⓕ 1 inch

   Ⓖ 3 inches

   Ⓗ 5 inches

   Ⓙ 7 inches

7. The ratio of the scale drawing of Brittany's family room to the actual family room is 1 inch to 5 feet. If the length of Brittany's family room is 20 feet, what should be the length of the family room on the scale drawing?

   Ⓐ 2 inches

   Ⓑ 6 inches

   Ⓒ 4 inches

   Ⓓ 8 inches

8. Fred's Building Company is designing a new volleyball court at Heritage High School. The ratio of the scale drawing to the actual court is 1 inch to 5 feet. If the length of the actual court will be 74 feet, what should be the length of the court on the scale drawing?

   Ⓕ 12.6 inches

   Ⓖ 14.8 inches

   Ⓗ 37.5 inches

   Ⓙ 74 inches

STOP

Name _____ Date _____

Mathematics

1.B

Using Inverse Relationships
Number and Operations

DIRECTIONS: Choose the best answer.

> **Examples:**
>
> An **inverse relationship** is when a pair of operations will undo each other.
>
> Addition and subtraction have an inverse relationship. For example, $2 + 3 = 5$ can also be reversed as $5 - 3 = 2$.
>
> Multiplication and division have an inverse relationship. For example: $2 \times 5 = 10$ can be reversed as $10 \div 5 = 2$.

 Clue Do not work the problems. Use the inverse relationships of addition/subtraction and multiplication/division to solve the problems.

1. If $28{,}153 - 17{,}745 = 10{,}408$, then $10{,}408 + 17{,}745 =$ _____ .
   - (A) 7,337
   - (B) 27,153
   - (C) 28,153
   - (D) 38,561

2. If $872 - 593 = 279$, then $279 + 593 =$ _____ .
   - (F) 872
   - (G) 314
   - (H) 593
   - (J) 558

3. If $x - 355 = y$, then $y + 355 =$ _____ .
   - (A) z
   - (B) y
   - (C) x
   - (D) none of the above

4. If $362 \times 16 = 5{,}792$, then $5{,}792 \div 16 =$ _____ .
   - (F) 462
   - (G) 362
   - (H) 1,362
   - (J) 92,192

5. If $a \times b = c$, then $c \div b =$ _____ .
   - (A) a
   - (B) b
   - (C) c
   - (D) x

6. If $x \div y = z$, then $z \times y =$ _____ .
   - (F) x^2
   - (G) y^2
   - (H) z^2
   - (J) none of the above

STOP

Mathematics

| 1.C |

Order of Operations
Number and Operations

DIRECTIONS: Follow the order of operations explained below to find the solutions. Show your work.

The order in which you do mathematical operations may change your answer. Mathematicians have agreed on a standard **order of operations.** The following phrase may help you remember the order. Each letter in the phrase stands for a mathematical operation.

Please	**P**arentheses
Excuse	**E**xponents
My	**M**ultiplication
Dear	**D**ivision
Aunt	**A**ddition
Sally	**S**ubtraction

1. $35 + 50 + \dfrac{25}{5} \times 5 - (8 + 11)$

2. $(-16 + 20) \times 6 \div (6 + 2) + 31$

3. $3 + 2(4 + 9 \div 3)$

4. $5 - [48 \div (12 + 4)] - 16$

5. $\dfrac{1}{2}(-16 - 4)$

6. $50 \div (4 \times 5 - 36 \div 2) + -9$

7. $4[-4(3 - 12) - 17]$

8. $[5(20 - 2)] \div \dfrac{30}{2} + 6 - 3$

9. $15 - 8 \times 2 + 11 - 5 \times 2$

10. $2^3 - 6 + [29 - 2 \times 3(1 + 4)]$

STOP

Mathematics

2.A

Generating Functions
Algebra

DIRECTIONS: Complete the table for each function rule given below.

Example:

Rule: $m = n + 3$

IN (n)	12	14	16	18	20	22
OUT (m)	15	17	19			

Answer: 21, 23, 25

1. Rule: $m = 3n$

IN (n)	0	1	2	3	4	5
OUT (m)						

2. Rule: $m = 3n - 3$

IN (n)	2	4	6	8	10	12
OUT (m)						

DIRECTIONS: Find the function rule for each table below.

3.

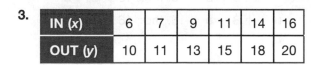

IN (x)	6	7	9	11	14	16
OUT (y)	10	11	13	15	18	20

Rule: $y = $ _____

4.

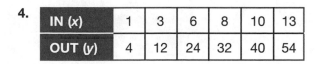

IN (x)	1	3	6	8	10	13
OUT (y)	4	12	24	32	40	54

Rule: $y = $ _____

5.

IN (x)	5	8	11	14	17	20
OUT (y)	3	6	9	12	15	18

Rule: $y = $ _____

6. Graph the ordered pairs for exercises 1, 3, and 5. Label each line using the rule.

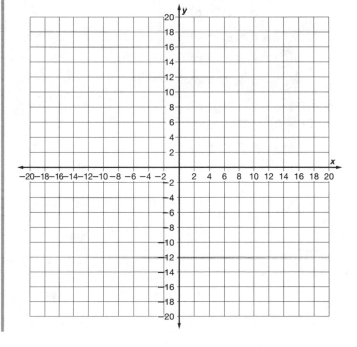

STOP

Mathematics

2.B

Using Variables
Algebra

DIRECTIONS: Choose the best answer.

 Clue A **variable** is an amount that is not known. It is often expressed by a letter.

1. $a \times (b + c) =$ _____
   - (A) $a \times b + a \times c$
   - (B) $a \times b + b \times c$
   - (C) $a \times b \times c$
   - (D) none of the above

2. $a + b =$ _____
   - (F) $b + c$
   - (G) $c + d$
   - (H) $b + a$
   - (J) $b - a$

3. $(a + b) + c =$ _____
   - (A) $c - (a + b)$
   - (B) $a + (b + c)$
   - (C) $a \times (b + c)$
   - (D) $a + (b \times c)$

4. $(a \times b) \times c =$ _____
   - (F) $a \times (b + c)$
   - (G) $a + (b \times c)$
   - (H) $a \times (b \times c)$
   - (J) $(a \times c) - b$

5. If $x > y$ and $y > z$, then _____ .
   - (A) $x < z$
   - (B) $x > z$
   - (C) $z > x$
   - (D) $x = z$

6. If $y > 98$ and $y < 123$, which of the following is a possible value of y?
   - (F) 124
   - (G) 108
   - (H) 97
   - (J) 221

7. Which statement is true if b is a whole number?
   - (A) If $b - 8 = 16$, then $8 + b = 16$
   - (B) If $8 \times b = 16$, then $16 \div b = 8$
   - (C) If $8 \div b = 16$, then $16 \times 8 = b$
   - (D) If $8 + b = 16$, then $16 + 8 = b$

STOP

Mathematics

2.B

Algebraic Expressions
Algebra

DIRECTIONS: Choose the best answer.

 Clue Look for key words, numbers, and figures in each problem. Be sure you perform the correct operation.

1. A desk normally costs $129. It is on sale for $99. How much would you save if you bought 2 desks on sale?

    (A)   ($129 + $99) × 2 = s

    (B)   ($129 − $99) ÷ 2 = s

    (C)   ($129 − $99) × 2 = s

    (D)   ($129 + $99) ÷ 2 = s

2. The highway department uses 6 gallons of paint for every 10 blocks of highway stripe. How many gallons will be needed for 250 blocks of highway stripe?

    (F)   (6 × 10) + 250 = g

    (G)   250 − (10 ÷ 6) = g

    (H)   250 × 10 × 6 = g

    (J)   (250 ÷ 10) × 6 = g

3. A hiker started out with 48 ounces of water. She drank 9 ounces of water after hiking 5 miles and 16 more when she reached mile marker 8. How many ounces of water did she have left?

    (A)   48 − (9 + 16) = w

    (B)   48 + (9 − 16) = w

    (C)   (16 − 9) + 48 = w

    (D)   48 + (9 + 16) = w

4. Evaluate $2a - 3b + 4c$, if $a = 4$, $b = 3$, and $c = 2$.

    (F)   25

    (G)   38

    (H)   7

    (J)   12

5. Evaluate $5g + 2h$, if $g = 1$ and $h = 4$.

    (A)   13

    (B)   28

    (C)   22

    (D)   7

6. A barrel is 36 inches from top to bottom. The water in the barrel is $12\frac{1}{2}$ inches deep. How much space is there from the surface of the water to the top of the barrel?

    (F) $s = 36 \div 12\frac{1}{2}$

    (G) $s = 36 \times 12\frac{1}{2}$

    (H) $s = 36 - 12\frac{1}{2}$

    (J) $s = 36 + 12\frac{1}{2}$

DIRECTIONS: Use the following information for question 7. The base of Sandy Mountain is 5,400 feet above sea level. The top of the mountain is 10,700 feet above sea level. A trail runs from the base of the mountain to the top. The trail is 8 miles long, and it takes about 5 hours to hike from the base of the mountain to the top.

7. Which of the following equations could be used to determine the vertical distance from the base of the mountain to the top?

    (A) $t - b = 5,300$

    (B) $t + b = 16,100$

    (C) $t \times b = 57,780,000$

    (D) $t \div b = 1.98$

STOP

Mathematics

| 2.C |

Solving One-Step Equations
Algebra

DIRECTIONS: Choose the best answer.

1. What is the value of z in the equation
   $12 \times z = 144$?

   (A) 8

   (B) 12

   (C) 122

   (D) 11

2. What is the value of x if $54 \div x = 9$?

   (F) 7

   (G) 6

   (H) 63

   (J) 45

3. What is the value of r if $17 \times r = 68$?

   (A) 51

   (B) 4

   (C) 85

   (D) 6

4. What is the value of a in the equation
   $a - 9 = 54$?

   (F) 45

   (G) 55

   (H) 63

   (J) 64

5. If $z + 8 = 31$, then $z =$

   (A) 39

   (B) 4

   (C) 22

   (D) 23

6. Your uncle bought 375 feet of wire fencing. He put up 325 feet today and saved the rest for tomorrow. Which equation shows how many feet of fencing he has left?

   (F) $375 + f = 325$

   (G) $375 - 325 = f$

   (H) $f = 375 + 325$

   (J) $375 - f = 325$

7. If 27 students each brought in 6 cookies, which equation shows how many cookies they brought in all?

   (A) $27 + 6 = c$

   (B) $27 \times 6 = c$

   (C) $27 - 6 = c$

   (D) $27 \div 6 = c$

8. Which equation shows the total attendance at the science fair if 67 girls and 59 boys attended?

   (F) $67 + 59 = a$

   (G) $67 - 59 = a$

   (H) $67 \div 59 = a$

   (J) $67 \times 59 = a$

9. Sergio spent $3.80 on heavy-duty string for his project. He bought 20 feet of string. Which equation could you use to find out the price per foot of the string?

   (A) $\$3.80 + 20 = s$

   (B) $\$3.80 - 20 = s$

   (C) $\$3.80 \times 20 = s$

   (D) $\$3.80 \div 20 = s$

STOP

Mathematics
| 2.D |

Changing Dimensions
Algebra

DIRECTIONS: Choose the best answer.

1. The plans for a park call for a rectangular pond measuring 300 feet wide by 100 feet long, with an area of 30,000 square feet. What would the area of the pond be if the length were increased to 300 feet?

  (A) 40,000 ft.^{2}
  (B) 60,000 ft.^{2}
  (C) 90,000 ft.^{2}
  (D) 24,000 ft.^{2}

2. For the pond described in question 1, what are the perimeters for both of the possible sizes?

  (F) 100 ft.; 300 ft.
  (G) 200 ft.; 600 ft.
  (H) 800 ft.; 1,200 ft.
  (J) 2,000 ft.; 2,400 ft.

3. If the perimeter of a plate with a diameter of 8 inches is 25.1 inches, what is the perimeter of a plate that is 2 inches larger in diameter?

  (A) 23.4 in.
  (B) 35.1 in.
  (C) 27.1 in.
  (D) 31.4 in.

4. A box of laundry detergent measures 12 inches high by 10 inches wide and 2 inches deep, and has a volume of 240 inches cubed. If the manufacturer wants to make a smaller box by decreasing each dimension by 1 inch, what would be the volume of the new box?

  (F) 99 in.^{3}
  (G) 120 in.^{3}
  (H) 21 in.^{3}
  (J) 84 in.^{3}

5. Look at the nested rectangles below. Use a table to determine the dimensions of the next larger rectangle.

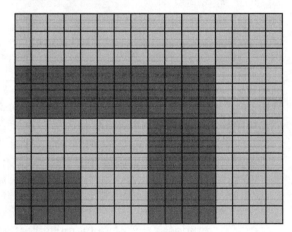

  (A) 20 × 15
  (B) 4 × 3
  (C) 16 × 12
  (D) 8 × 6

Mathematics
1.0–2.0
For pages 44–53

Mini-Test 1

Number and Operations; Algebra

DIRECTIONS: Use this information for question 1. There are 4 apples, 2 bananas, 5 oranges, and 3 pears in a fruit bowl.

1. **What is the ratio of apples to oranges?**

   Ⓐ 5:4

   Ⓑ $\frac{4}{5}$

   Ⓒ 4 to 14

   Ⓓ $\frac{9}{5}$

DIRECTIONS: Choose the best answer.

2. **What are all the prime factors of 12?**

   Ⓕ 2, 3, and 4

   Ⓖ 24, 36, and 48

   Ⓗ 2 and 6

   Ⓙ 2 and 3

3. **Which of the following correctly lists the order of mathematical operations?**

   Ⓐ parentheses, exponents, division, multiplication, addition, subtraction

   Ⓑ multiplication, division, addition, subtraction, parentheses, exponents

   Ⓒ parentheses, exponents, multiplication, division, addition, subtraction

   Ⓓ exponents, parentheses, multiplication, division, addition, subtraction

4. **Kinesha wants to frame an 8 inch by 10 inch picture with a 3 inch mat. What size frame does she need?**

   Ⓕ 8" × 10"

   Ⓖ 9" × 11"

   Ⓗ 14" × 16"

   Ⓙ 30" × 32"

5. **Mrs. Wacker looked at the chart below to determine how many ounces of chocolate mint sauce she needed to prepare for the vanilla bean pie her guests will enjoy at her dinner party.**

Servings	1	2	3	4	5
Ounces of Sauce Needed	2	4	6	8	10

Mrs. Wacker has invited 6 guests who will each get 1 serving of her famous dessert. She also plans to make 12 extra ounces of sauce to give to one of the guests to take home. Which expression can be used to determine how many ounces of chocolate mint sauce Mrs. Wacker needs to make?

   Ⓐ 12 + (2 × 6)

   Ⓑ (12 + 2) × 6

   Ⓒ (2 × 12) + (8 × 6)

   Ⓓ 6 × (2 + 8) + 12

6. **Which of the following expressions is equal to the expression: $2(3c - 1)$?**

   Ⓕ $3c - 2$

   Ⓖ $23c - 2$

   Ⓗ $6c - 2$

   Ⓙ $6c - 1$

DIRECTIONS: Complete the table for the function rule given below.

7. **Rule: $m = n + 3$**

IN(n)	12	14	16	18	20	22
OUT(m)	15	17	19			

STOP

Mathematics

3.A

Classifying Quadrilaterals
Geometry

DIRECTIONS: Give the name for each quadrilateral. Then, find each missing angle measurement.

Name	Description	Example
trapezoid	• 1 pair of opposite sides are parallel	
parallelogram	• opposite sides are parallel • opposite sides and opposite angles are congruent	
rhombus	• parallelogram with all sides congruent	
rectangle	• parallelogram with four right angles	
square	• rectangle with four congruent sides	

Clue The sum of the measures of the angles in any quadrilateral is 360°.

1.

_____

2.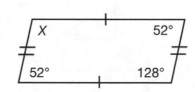

_____

3.

_____

4.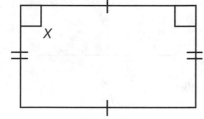

_____

5.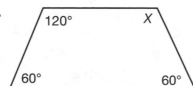

_____

6.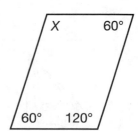

_____

STOP

Mathematics

3.A

Classifying Polyhedrons
Geometry

DIRECTIONS: Under each shape below, write *prism, pyramid,* or *neither* to show what type of 3-dimensional object it is.

Examples:

Prisms are 3-dimensional shapes with the following characteristics:
- two opposite, identical bases shaped like polygons
- rectangular faces

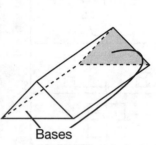

Bases

Bases

Pyramids are 3-dimensional shapes with the following characteristics:
- one base shaped like a polygon
- triangular faces
- a point on one end

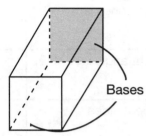

Base

Point

Point

Base

1.

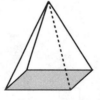

_____

2.

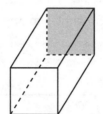

_____

3.

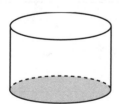

_____

4.

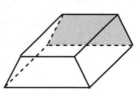

_____

5.

_____

6.

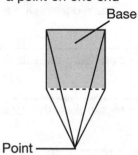

_____

7.

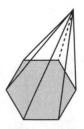

_____

8.

_____

9.

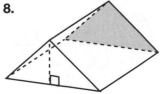

_____

STOP

Name _____   Date _____

Mathematics

3.B

Using a Coordinate System
Geometry

DIRECTIONS: Write the coordinate pairs for each figure plotted.

Points on a graph are labeled using coordinate pairs. The first value in the pair represents the horizontal distance from zero. A positive number means to move right. A negative number means to move left. The second value in the pair represents the vertical distance from zero. A positive number means to move up. A negative number means to move down.

Look at the example point graphed on the grid below. This point is 5 units to the left of zero and 4 units above zero. Therefore, it would be labeled (−5, 4). The point (−5, 4) is called a **coordinate pair** or an **ordered pair**.

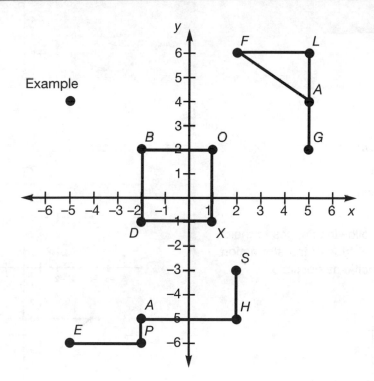

1. FLAG

F = (,   )

L = (,   )

A = (,   )

G = (,   )

2. BOXD

B = (,   )

O = (,   )

X = (,   )

D = (,   )

3. SHAPE

S = (,   )

H = (,   )

A = (,   )

P = (,   )

E = (,   )

STOP

Mathematics

3.C

Analyzing Transformations
Geometry

DIRECTIONS: Choose the best answer.

1. **Parallelogram *QRST* slid to a new position on the grid as shown. Which moves describe the slide?**

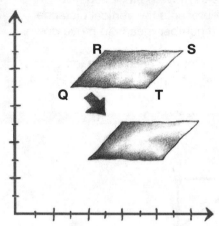

(A)   1 right, 4 down

(B)   1 right, 5 down

(C)   2 right, 4 down

(D)   1 right, 3 down

DIRECTIONS: Compare the following images to their transformation images. What type of transformation was performed? Be as specific as possible.

2.

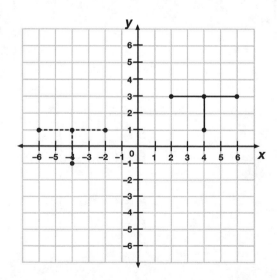

_____

3.

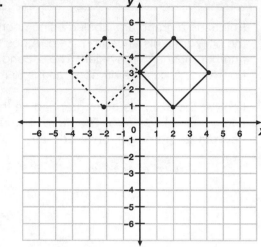

_____

4.

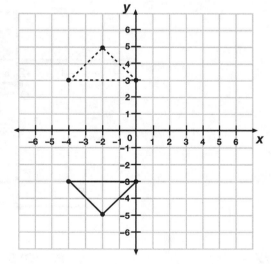

_____

STOP

Mathematics

| 3.C |

Rotational and Line Symmetry
Geometry

DIRECTIONS: Write *yes* beneath each object that has rotational symmetry and *no* beneath objects that do not have rotational symmetry.

To check if an object has rotational symmetry, follow these steps.
- Trace the object using a small square of tracing paper.
- Place the traced image on top of the original image. Hold the traced image by a pencil-point in the center of the image.
- Rotate your tracing paper around the center point. If the traced image matches exactly with the original image before you have rotated the paper in one full circle, then the shape has rotational symmetry.

1.

_____

2.

_____

3.

_____

4.

_____

5.

_____

6.

_____

DIRECTIONS: Draw dotted lines to represent the lines of symmetry on polygons that have reflection symmetry. A polygon may have more than one line of symmetry. If there are no lines of symmetry, write *none* below the shape.

7.

8.

9.

10.
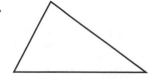

11.

12.
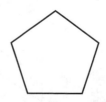

Name _____ Date _____

Finding the Volume of Three Dimensional Models
Geometry

DIRECTIONS: Choose the best answer.

 Clue Find the volume of each space figure by counting the cubes.

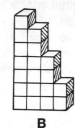

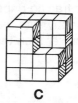

| A | B | C | D |

1. What is the volume of Shape A?

- (A) 38
- (B) 14
- (C) 42
- (D) 50

2. What is the volume of Shape B?

- (F) 38
- (G) 19
- (H) 10
- (J) 26

3. What is the volume of Shape C?

- (A) 26
- (B) 16
- (C) 32
- (D) 28

4. What is the volume of Shape D?

- (F) 48
- (G) 46
- (H) 40
- (J) 38

DIRECTIONS: Find the volume of the following rectangular prisms. Include the appropriate units in your answer.

5.

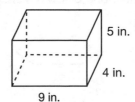

5 in.
4 in.
9 in.

Volume: _____

7.

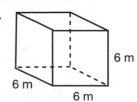

6 m
6 m
6 m

Volume: _____

6.

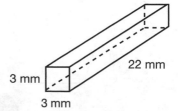

22 mm
3 mm
3 mm

Volume: _____

8.

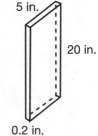

5 in.
20 in.
0.2 in.

Volume: _____

STOP

Mathematics

4.A

Identifying Equivalent Units of Measure
Measurement

DIRECTIONS: Choose the best answer.

1. **A recipe calls for 6 quarts of water. How many gallons is that?**

   (A) 1 gallon

   (B) $1\frac{1}{2}$ gallons

   (C) 2 gallons

   (D) $2\frac{1}{2}$ gallons

2. **Kenny's book is 30 mm thick. How many centimeters thick is the book?**

   (F) 0.3 cm

   (G) 3 cm

   (H) 33 cm

   (J) 300 cm

3. **1 kilogram = _____**

   (A) 100 milligrams

   (B) 10 grams

   (C) 100 grams

   (D) 1,000 grams

4. **A hair comb weighs about 35 grams. How many milligrams does that equal?**

   (F) 3.5 milligrams

   (G) 35,000 milligrams

   (H) 350 milligrams

   (J) 3,500 milligrams

5. **30 ft. = _____**

   (A) 5 yd.

   (B) 10 yd.

   (C) 15 yd.

   (D) 20 yd.

6. **A football field is 100 yards long. About how many inches is that?**

   (F) 800 inches

   (G) 3,600 inches

   (H) 33 inches

   (J) 400 inches

7. **4 gallons = _____**

   (A) 40 cups

   (B) 8 quarts

   (C) 16 pints

   (D) 64 cups

8. **16 cups is equivalent to all of the following except _____ .**

   (F) 8 pints

   (G) 1 gallon

   (H) 4 quarts

   (J) 100 fluid ounces

STOP

Mathematics

| 4.B |

Circumference and
Area of Circles
Measurement

DIRECTIONS: Find the circumference and area of each circle below. Include the appropriate units in your answer.

Example:

The **circumference** of a circle is the distance around the outside of the circle.
$C = \pi d$, where d = diameter

The **area** of a circle is the space inside the circle.
$A = \pi r^2$, where r = radius

$\pi = 3.14$

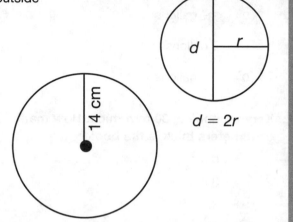

$d = 2r$

$d = 2r = 2 \times 14 = 28$ cm
$C = \pi d = 3.14 \times 28 = 87.92$ cm
$A = \pi r^2 = 3.14 \times 14^2 = 3.14 \times 196 = 615.44$ cm^2

1.

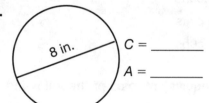

8 in.

C = _____
A = _____

2.

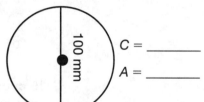

100 mm

C = _____
A = _____

3.

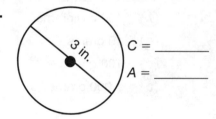

3 in.

C = _____
A = _____

4.

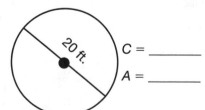

20 ft.

C = _____
A = _____

5.

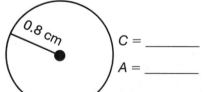

0.8 cm

C = _____
A = _____

6.

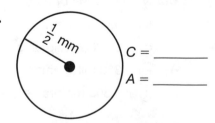

$\frac{1}{2}$ mm

C = _____
A = _____

7.

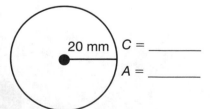

20 mm

C = _____
A = _____

8.

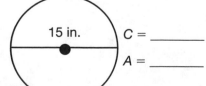

15 in.

C = _____
A = _____

9.

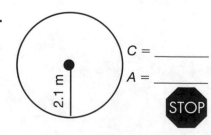

2.1 m

C = _____
A = _____

STOP

Name _____   Date _____

Finding the Measurement
of Unknown Angles
Measurement

DIRECTIONS: Look at each triangle. Write the type of triangle (*right*, *acute* or *obtuse*) on the line. Then, write the measurement of the missing angle. The first one is done for you.

Clue The angle measures in a triangle always add up to 180°. The angle measures in any quadrilateral always add up to 360°.

1.
30°
right 60°

2.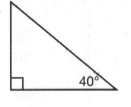
45°
25°
_____

3.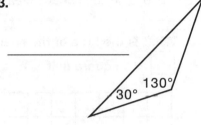
_____
30° 130°

4.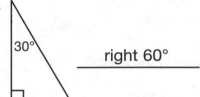
70°
60°
_____

5.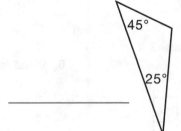
40°
_____

6.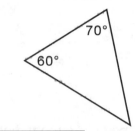
49°
60°
_____

DIRECTIONS: Find each missing angle measurement.

7.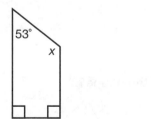
53°
x
_____

8.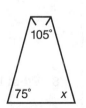
105°
75°   x
_____

9.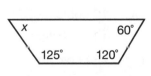
x   60°
125°   120°
_____

10.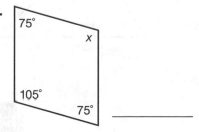
75°
x
105°
75°   _____

11.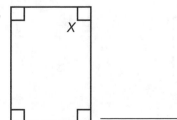
X
_____

12.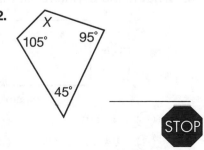
X
105°   95°
45°
_____

STOP

Mathematics

4.B

Finding Perimeter, Area, and Volume
Measurement

DIRECTIONS: Choose the best answer.

1. The measure of the amount of liquid a glass can hold is called its _____ .

   (A) volume

   (B) capacity

   (C) circumference

   (D) inside surface area

2. What is the area of the shaded shape?

   ☐ = 1 square unit

   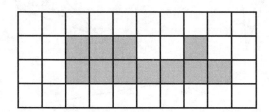

   (F) 9 square units

   (G) 8 square units

   (H) 11 square units

   (J) 22 square units

3. What is the volume of a rectangular prism with a length of 8 feet, a height of 6 feet, and width of 2 feet?

   (A) 16 cubic feet

   (B) 18 cubic feet

   (C) 96 cubic feet

   (D) 32 cubic feet

4. What is the perimeter of this rectangle?

   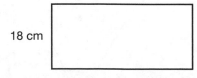

   (F) 42 cm   (H) 432 cm

   (G) 84 cm   (J) 82 cm

5. A shoebox is 6 inches wide, 11 inches long, and 5 inches high. What is the volume of the box?

   (A) 330 cubic inches

   (B) 22 cubic inches

   (C) 230 cubic inches

   (D) none of these

6. What is the area of the shape?

   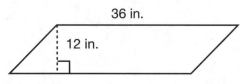

   (F) 532 in.^{2}

   (G) 432 in.^{2}

   (H) 48 in.^{2}

   (J) 96 in.^{2}

7. What is the perimeter of a room that measures 12 feet by 19 feet?

   (A) 31 feet

   (B) 43 feet

   (C) 62 feet

   (D) 228 feet

8. What is the area of the shape?

   (F) 2 cm^2

   (G) 4 cm^2

   (H) 8 cm^2

   (J) 16 cm^2

   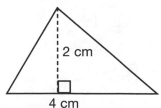

STOP

Mathematics

3.0–4.0

For pages 55–64

Mini-Test 2

Geometry; Measurement

DIRECTIONS: Compare the following image to its transformation image. What type of transformation was performed? Be as specific as possible.

1.

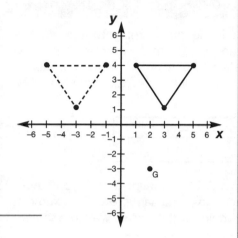

_____

2. **In the graph above, what are the coordinates for point G?**

(A) (2, 3)

(B) (2, –3)

(C) (3, 2)

(D) (–3, 2)

3. **Which figure is a pyramid?**

1 2 3 ▲

(F) Figure 1

(G) Figure 2

(H) Figure 3

(J) none of the above

4. **What is the volume of a rectangular prism with a length of 6 feet, a height of 4 feet, and a width of 3 feet?**

(A) 36 cubic feet

(B) 288 cubic feet

(C) 72 cubic feet

(D) 216 cubic feet

5. **What is the area of this circle?**

(F) 31.4 in.^{2}

(G) 62.8 in.^{2}

(H) 78.5 in.^{2}

(J) 314 in.^{2}

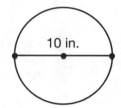

10 in.

6. **What is the missing measure in this triangle?**

(A) 30°

(B) 50°

(C) 60°

(D) 90°

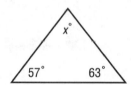

$x°$

57°   63°

7. **Draw and name a polygon with four sides and four right angles. Opposite sides are parallel.**

STOP

Mathematics

5.A

Using Stem and Leaf Plots
Data Analysis and Probability

DIRECTIONS: Make a stem and leaf plot for the following data. Ms. Jensen's class completed a math test. The test scores out of 50 possible points were 49, 35, 37, 47, 43, 50, 44, 45, 48, 38, 41, 50, 45, and 50.

Example:

To use a stem and leaf plot, each value in the data is split into a "stem" and a "leaf." The "leaf" is most often the last digit of the number. The other digits to the left of the "leaf" are the "stem." For example, in the number 214, the "stem" would be 21 and the "leaf" would be 4. You can show this in a table, such as this:

Stem	Leaf
21	4

The legend for the table would be: Legend: 21 | 4 means 214. If you have multiple entries, the leaves for each stem go in the same row. For example, the data 214, 216, 223, 217, and 224 would be shown this way in a table:

Stem	Leaf
21	4, 6, 7
22	3, 4

Math Test Scores (out of 50 points)	
Stem	**Leaf**

Legend: 3 | 5 means 35

To find the median in a stem and leaf plot, count off half the total number of leaves.

What is the median grade for the math test? _____

STOP

Mathematics

5.B

Mean, Median, Mode, and Range
Data Analysis and Probability

DIRECTIONS: For each store, calculate the mean, median, mode, and range of prices for soccer cleats. All prices have been rounded to the nearest dollar.

Mean: average number
Median: middle number of ordered data
Mode: the value that occurs most often
Range: the difference between the largest and smallest values

1. Store 1 Prices

$45 $32
$45 $70 $45
$20 $48 $55
$50 $32

Mean:_____

Median:_____

Mode:_____

Range:_____

2. Store 2 Prices

$35 $40
$35 $25 $75
$50 $63 $80
$42 $35

Mean:_____

Median:_____

Mode:_____

Range:_____

3. Store 3 Prices

$85 $50 $45
$60 $45 $80
$85 $20 $85
$50 $100

Mean:_____

Median:_____

Mode:_____

Range:_____

4. Store 4 Prices

$55 $60
$88 $60 $32
$80 $48 $64
$80 $60

Mean:_____

Median:_____

Mode:_____

Range:_____

DIRECTIONS: Answer the following questions on another sheet of paper. Write your answers in complete sentences.

5. Store 3 claims they have shoes to fit any budget, since they have the largest range of prices. Look at the data for Store 3. Do you agree they have the best variety of prices? Explain.

6. Which store has the lowest average price?

7. If you wanted to find the store with the best variety of low-priced shoes, which would you choose? Which "middle number" could help you make this decision?

STOP

Mathematics

5.C

Effect of Sample
Size on Probabilities

Data Analysis and Probability

DIRECTIONS: Answer the following questions.

1. What is the theoretical probability of randomly picking a face card from a standard 52-card deck?

   (A) $\frac{1}{52}$

   (B) $\frac{12}{52}$

   (C) $\frac{2}{5}$

   (D) $\frac{1}{2}$

2. Jose randomly picks a card from a standard 52-card deck and selects the 9 of hearts. He puts the card back into the deck and picks again. This time, he selects the queen of clubs. From this experiment, he can predict that the empirical probability of randomly picking a face card from a standard 52-card deck is _____ .

   (F) $\frac{1}{52}$

   (G) $\frac{12}{52}$

   (H) $\frac{2}{5}$

   (J) $\frac{1}{2}$

3. Suppose instead of picking cards from the deck twice, as described in question 2, Jose picks cards 100 times. What do you think the effect will be on his prediction of the empirical probability of randomly picking a face card from the deck?

   _____

   _____

   _____

   _____

   _____

   _____

   _____

   _____

   _____

   _____

   _____

   _____

   _____

STOP

Mathematics

5.D

Listing Outcomes
Data Analysis and Probability

DIRECTIONS: Draw a tree diagram or make a list to show all the outcomes.

Example:

A tree diagram shows all possible outcomes. For example, if a car can be ordered in black, red, or tan and the seats can be leather or fabric, the possible outcomes can be shown as follows:

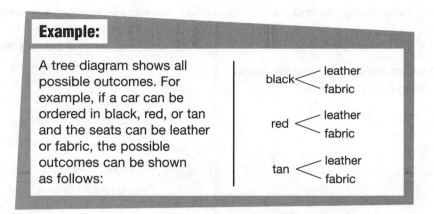

1. Phones come in two styles: wall and desk. They come in four colors: red, white, black, and beige. Show the outcomes.

2. The lunch room serves 3 types of fruit, 4 types of vegetables, and 2 types of meat. How many different combinations can be made from these choices? Draw the tree diagram to show all the outcomes.

3. Arapaho sees an ad in the newspaper for a sale at the Rain on Your Parade clothing store. Sundresses are selling for $35.88 each. Bonnets have dropped to the unbeatable price of 2 for $5.99, and sandals have slipped to $23.48 a pair. If Arapaho buys 2 sundresses, 6 bonnets, and 3 pairs of sandals, draw a tree diagram that shows how many outfits she can make with her purchases.

STOP

| 6.A/6.B |

Solving Problems
Process

DIRECTIONS: Choose the best answer.

1. Matthew spent $\frac{1}{2}$ hour doing his history homework and $\frac{3}{4}$ hour doing his science homework. Which equation shows how much time he spent doing his homework?

    (A) $\frac{1}{2} \times \frac{3}{4} = t$

    (B) $\frac{3}{4} \div \frac{1}{2} = t$

    (C) $\frac{1}{2} + \frac{3}{4} = t$

    (D) $\frac{1}{2} - \frac{3}{4} = t$

2. A store is open for 12 hours a day. Each hour, an average of 15 customers come into the store. Which equation shows how many customers come into the store in a day?

    (F) $15 \times 24 = c$

    (G) $12 + 15 = c$

    (H) $12 \times 15 = c$

    (J) $24 \div 12 = c$

3. There are 24 people at a meeting. Suppose $\frac{2}{3}$ of the people are women. Which equation shows how many are men?

    (A) $16 - \left(\frac{2}{3} \times 24 \right) = m$

    (B) $24 - \left(\frac{1}{3} \times 24 \right) = m$

    (C) $24 \times \frac{2}{3} - 4 = m$

    (D) $24 \times \frac{1}{3} = m$

4. Angelica is helping her dad build a deck. The surface of the deck will be 12 feet wide and 14 feet long. The boards they are using can cover an area of 4 square feet each. Which of these shows how many boards they will need to cover the surface of the deck?

    (F) $(12 \times 14) \div 4 = \blacksquare$

    (G) $(12 \times 14) \times 4 = \blacksquare$

    (H) $12 + 14 + 4 = \blacksquare$

    (J) $(12 \div 14) \times 4 = \blacksquare$

DIRECTIONS: For questions 5–6, imagine that the temperature in Rockville at 7:00 A.M. was −7°C. By 12:00 noon, the temperature increased to 13°C, but it fell by 3°C by 6:00 P.M.

5. How much did the temperature increase between 7:00 A.M. and 12:00 noon?

    (A) 6°C

    (B) 20°C

    (C) −6°C

    (D) −20°C

6. What is the average hourly temperature gain between 7:00 A.M. and 12:00 noon?

    (F) −4°C

    (G) 20°C

    (H) 4°C

    (J) −20°C

STOP

Name _____   Date _____

Mathematics

6.C

Using Mathematical Language
Process

DIRECTIONS: Choose the best answer.

1. The point where two sides of an angle meet is called _____ .
   - (A) the vertex
   - (B) the circumference
   - (C) an acute angle
   - (D) a ray

2. A plane figure with 6 sides is called _____ .
   - (F) an apex
   - (G) an octagon
   - (H) a hexagon
   - (J) a pentagon

3. The measure of the amount of liquid a glass can hold is called its _____ .
   - (A) volume
   - (B) capacity
   - (C) circumference
   - (D) inside surface area

4. What is not shown in the diagram?
   - (F) parallel lines
   - (G) intersecting lines
   - (H) line segment
   - (J) perpendicular lines

5. What fraction of a pound is 4 ounces?
   - (A) $\frac{1}{8}$
   - (B) $\frac{1}{4}$
   - (C) $\frac{1}{2}$
   - (D) $\frac{1}{5}$

6. A map scale shows that 1 inch equals 8 miles. About how long would a section of highway be that is 4.5 inches on the map?
   - (F) 36 miles
   - (G) 32.5 miles
   - (H) 30 miles
   - (J) 18 miles

7. Which unit of measure would be best to use when weighing an adult elephant?
   - (A) pounds
   - (B) grams
   - (C) kilograms
   - (D) tons

8. A cube has a side that measures 25 centimeters. What is the total volume of the cube?
   - (F) 15,625 cubic cm
   - (G) 625 cubic cm
   - (H) 300 cubic cm
   - (J) 50 cubic cm

25 centimeters

STOP

Mathematics

| 6.D |

Applying Math to Other Areas
Process

___

DIRECTIONS: Choose the best answer.

Mr. Vander's class earned $582 during the school year to purchase new books for the library. The graph below shows the percentage of money earned from each activity. Use it to answer questions 1–3.

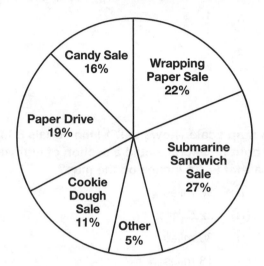

1. **Which fund-raiser earned the most money?**

   (A)　the candy sale

   (B)　the wrapping paper sale

   (C)　the submarine sandwich sale

   (D)　the paper drive

2. **How much less was earned on the paper drive than from the wrapping paper sale?**

   (F)　$17.46

   (G)　$23.46

   (H)　$18.46

   (J)　$16.46

3. **How much money was earned from the cookie dough sale?**

   (A)　$63.02

   (B)　$123.02

   (C)　$64.02

   (D)　$73.03

DIRECTIONS: The soccer team members needed to buy their own shin guards, socks, shoes, and shorts. Two players volunteered to do some comparative shopping to find the store with the best deals. Use their charts to answer questions 4 and 5.

Sports Corner

Socks	3 pairs for $9.30
Shoes	2 pairs for $48.24
Shin Guards	4 pairs for $32.48
Shorts	5 pairs for $60.30

4. **How much would it cost to buy one pair of shoes and socks at Sports Corner?**

   (F)　$27.22

   (G)　$57.54

   (H)　$31.47

   (J)　$28.22

Sam's Soccer Corner

Socks	2 pairs for $6.84
Shoes	3 pairs for $84.15
Shin Guards	5 pairs for $35.70
Shorts	4 pairs for $36.36

5. **How much would it cost to buy one pair of shoes and socks at Sam's Soccer Supplies?**

   (A)　$27.22

   (B)　$31.47

   (C)　$29.11

   (D)　$31.57

STOP

Communicating
Mathematical Ideas
Process

DIRECTIONS: Choose the best answer.

1. **What number completes this number sentence?**

$$4 \times 35 = 4 \times (\blacksquare + 5)$$

- (A) 35
- (B) 30
- (C) 3
- (D) 38

2. **Lizette makes cubes from blocks to display as shown below. How many blocks will she use to make Display 6?**

Display 1   Display 2   Display 3

- (F) 36 blocks
- (G) 64 blocks
- (H) 125 blocks
- (J) 216 blooks

3. **What is the perimeter of this rectangle?**

- (A) 33 cm
- (B) 60 cm
- (C) 66 cm
- (D) 68 cm

6 cm ☐
27 cm

4. **How many more glass balls are needed to fill the box to the top?**

- (F) 20 balls
- (G) 22 balls
- (H) 24 balls
- (J) 26 balls

5. **About how much will the popcorn on the scale cost?**

68¢ a pound
$1.18 a pound
58¢ a pound
78¢ a pound
98¢ a pound

- (A) $1.80
- (B) $2.50
- (C) $3.25
- (D) $4.95

6. **Nako is using nickels to measure the area of a dollar bill. About how many nickels will it take to cover the dollar bill?**

- (F) about 50
- (G) about 21
- (H) about 18
- (J) about 10

7. **About how long is the paper clip above the ruler?**

centimeters

1 2 3 4 5 6 7 8

- (A) 3.5 cm
- (B) 4 cm
- (C) 4.5 cm
- (D) 5 cm

STOP

Name _____   Date _____

Mini-Test 3

Data Analysis and Probability; Process

DIRECTIONS: Use the data set for questions 1–3. The test scores for a class are 86, 94, 70, 81, 92, 74, 75, 89, 76, and 97.

1. **What is the mean of the data?**
   - (A) 27
   - (B) 83.4
   - (C) 83.5
   - (D) none of the above

2. **What is the median of the data?**
   - (F) 27
   - (G) 83.4
   - (H) 83.5
   - (J) none of the above

3. **Create a stem and leaf plot using the data set.**

Stem	Leaf

DIRECTIONS: Choose the best answer.

4. **The sweaters on sale come in three styles: pullover, cardigan, and turtleneck. They come in three colors: black, white, and red. How many possible outcomes are there?**
   - (A) 9
   - (B) 6
   - (C) 3
   - (D) 12

5. **If you try to guess the month someone was born, what is the probability that you will guess the correct month?**
   - (F) $\frac{1}{12}$
   - (G) $\frac{1}{6}$
   - (H) $\frac{1}{24}$
   - (J) $\frac{1}{13}$

6. **Diane has been hired by the supermarket as a part-time worker. She will earn $5.50 an hour, and she will work 12 hours each week. How much will she earn in a week?**
   - (A) $66.00
   - (B) $56.50
   - (C) $17.50
   - (D) $60.50

DIRECTIONS: Use the graph below to answer question 7.

7. **About 16 million people live in Florida. About how many of them live in cities?**

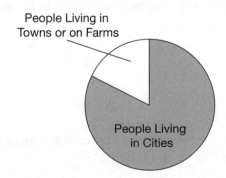

People Living in Towns or on Farms

People Living in Cities

   - (F) 14 million
   - (G) 8 million
   - (H) 5 million
   - (J) 3 million

STOP

How Am I Doing?

Mini-Test 1

Page 54

Number Correct

7 answers correct	**Great Job!** Move on to the section test on page 76.
5–6 answers correct	**You're almost there!** But you still need a little practice. Review practice pages 44–53 before moving on to the section test on page 76.
0–4 answers correct	**Oops!** Time to review what you have learned and try again. Review the practice section on pages 44–53. Then, retake the test on page 54. Now, move on to the section test on page 76.

Mini-Test 2

Page 65

Number Correct

7 answers correct	**Awesome!** Move on to the section test on page 76.
5–6 answers correct	**You're almost there!** But you still need a little practice. Review practice pages 55–64 before moving on to the section test on page 76.
0–4 answers correct	**Oops!** Time to review what you have learned and try again. Review the practice section on pages 55–64. Then, retake the test on page 65. Now, move on to the section test on page 76.

Mini-Test 3

Page 74

Number Correct

7 answers correct	**Great Job!** Move on to the section test on page 76.
5–6 answers correct	**You're almost there!** But you still need a little practice. Review practice pages 66–73 before moving on to the section test on page 76.
0–4 answers correct	**Oops!** Time to review what you have learned and try again. Review the practice section on pages 66–73. Then, retake the test on page 74. Now, move on to the section test on page 76.

Final Mathematics Test
for pages 44–73

DIRECTIONS: Choose the best answer.

1. **Which of the following are the prime factors for 30?**

   Ⓐ 10×3

   Ⓑ 15×2

   Ⓒ 5×6

   Ⓓ $3 \times 5 \times 2$

DIRECTIONS: The chart below shows how the space in a store was divided among the different departments. Use the chart to answer questions 2–3.

2. **If the total space in the store is 3,000 square feet, how many square feet of space is taken up by packaged foods?**

   Ⓕ 400 square feet

   Ⓖ 550 square feet

   Ⓗ 600 square feet

   Ⓙ 60 square feet

3. **What fraction of the space is the bakery?**

   Ⓐ $\frac{1}{4}$

   Ⓑ $\frac{1}{8}$

   Ⓒ $\frac{1}{5}$

   Ⓓ $\frac{1}{10}$

DIRECTIONS: Choose the best answer.

4. **Which of the tables follows this rule?**

   Rule: Multiply the number in column A by 24 to get the number in column B.

   Ⓕ

A	B
2	36
3	42
5	54
7	66

   Ⓗ

A	B
2	12
3	16
5	15
7	17

   Ⓖ

A	B
2	16
3	22
5	34
7	46

   Ⓙ

A	B
2	48
3	72
5	120
7	168

5. **Jacob has a bag with 13 pieces of candy. His father puts some more candy into the bag. He now has 28 pieces. Which equation shows how many pieces his father gave him?**

   Ⓐ $28 \div 13 = \blacksquare$

   Ⓑ $13 + \blacksquare = 28$

   Ⓒ $28 \times 13 = \blacksquare$

   Ⓓ $13 - \blacksquare = 28$

6. **What is the value of y if $y + 15 = 87$?**

   Ⓕ 72

   Ⓖ 82

   Ⓗ 92

   Ⓙ 102

GO

7. 75,000 g = _____

(A) 7.5 kg

(B) 75 kg

(C) 750 kg

(D) 7,500 kg

8. **Which of the following figures is a trapezoid?**

(F)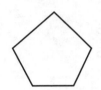

(G)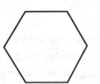

(H)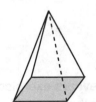

(J)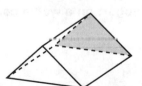

9. **Which of the following is not a prism?**

(A)

(B)

(C)

(D)

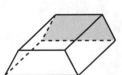

10. **A box is 7 inches wide, 10 inches long, and 5 inches high. Find the volume of the box.**

(F) 350 cubic inches

(G) 22 cubic inches

(H) 700 cubic inches

(J) 70 cubic inches

11. **Which of these are the coordinates of the triangle?**

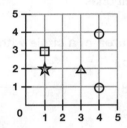

(A) (1, 2)

(B) (3, 2)

(C) (1, 3)

(D) (4, 4)

12. **Which of the following figures does not have a line of symmetry?**

(F)

(G)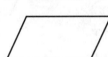

(H)

(J)

GO

13. Daniel is using a scale drawing to design his dream house. The ratio for the scale drawing to the actual house is 1 inch to 3 feet. If the length of the actual living room will be 24 feet, what should the length of the living room be on the scale drawing?

Ⓐ 5 inches

Ⓑ 8 inches

Ⓒ 12 inches

Ⓓ 2.4 inches

14. What is the area of a circle with a radius of 2?

Ⓕ 50.24

Ⓖ 6.28

Ⓗ 12.56

Ⓙ 25.12

15. What is the circumference of a circle with a diameter of 4?

Ⓐ 50.24

Ⓑ 6.28

Ⓒ 12.56

Ⓓ 25.12

DIRECTIONS: Write the measurement of the missing angle.

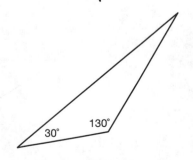

16. Ⓕ 20°

Ⓖ 310°

Ⓗ 110°

Ⓙ 70°

17. Ⓐ 20°

Ⓑ 100°

Ⓒ 200°

Ⓓ 160°

18. Find the mode for 85, 105, 135, 85, and 65.

Ⓕ 70

Ⓖ 85

Ⓗ 86

Ⓙ 95

19. Find the median for 85, 105, 135, 85, and 65.

Ⓐ 70

Ⓑ 85

Ⓒ 86

Ⓓ 95

20. Find the mean for 85, 105, 135, 85, 65, 80, and 84.

Ⓕ 70

Ⓖ 85

Ⓗ 86

Ⓙ 91.3

21. The convenience store has a choice of chocolate, vanilla, and strawberry frozen yogurt in either a sugar cone or a waffle cone. How many choices are there?

Ⓐ 9

Ⓑ 6

Ⓒ 3

Ⓓ 5

22. For the previous exercise, what is the probability that you will choose a chocolate frozen yogurt on a waffle cone?

Ⓕ $\frac{1}{3}$

Ⓖ $\frac{1}{5}$

Ⓗ $\frac{1}{6}$

Ⓙ $\frac{1}{9}$

STOP

Final Mathematics Test

Answer Sheet

1 (A) (B) (C) (D)
2 (F) (G) (H) (J)
3 (A) (B) (C) (D)
4 (F) (G) (H) (J)
5 (A) (B) (C) (D)
6 (F) (G) (H) (J)
7 (A) (B) (C) (D)
8 (F) (G) (H) (J)
9 (A) (B) (C) (D)
10 (F) (G) (H) (J)

11 (A) (B) (C) (D)
12 (F) (G) (H) (J)
13 (A) (B) (C) (D)
14 (F) (G) (H) (J)
15 (A) (B) (C) (D)
16 (F) (G) (H) (J)
17 (A) (B) (C) (D)
18 (F) (G) (H) (J)
19 (A) (B) (C) (D)
20 (F) (G) (H) (J)

21 (A) (B) (C) (D)
22 (F) (G) (H) (J)

Social Studies Standards

Standard 1—Culture *(See pages 81–83.)*
Social studies programs should include experiences that provide for the study of culture and cultural diversity.

Standard 2—Time, Continuity, and Change *(See pages 84–85.)*
Social studies programs should include experiences that provide for the study of the way human beings view themselves in and over time.

Standard 3—People, Places, and Environments *(See pages 86–87.)*
Social studies programs should include experiences that provide for the study of people, places, and environments.

Standard 4—Individual Development and Identity *(See pages 89–90.)*
Social studies programs should include experiences that provide for the study of individual development and identity.

Standard 5—Individuals, Groups, and Institutions *(See pages 91–92.)*
Social studies programs should include experiences that provide for the study of individuals, groups, and institutions.

Standard 6—Power, Authority, and Governance *(See pages 94–95.)*
Social studies programs should include experiences that provide for the study of how people create and change structures of power, authority, and governance.

Standard 7—Production, Distribution, and Consumption *(See pages 96–98.)*
Social studies programs should include experiences that provide for the study of how people organize for the production, distribution, and consumption of goods and services.

Standard 8—Science, Technology, and Society *(See page 99.)*
Social studies programs should include experiences that provide for the study of relationships among science, technology, and society.

Standard 9—Global Connections *(See pages 101–102.)*
Social studies programs should include experiences that provide for the study of global connections and interdependence.

Standard 10—Civic Ideals and Practices *(See pages 103–104.)*
Social studies programs should include experiences that provide for the study of the ideals, principles, and practices of citizenship in a democratic republic.

Social Studies

[1.0]

Cultural Diversity in the United States
Culture

DIRECTIONS: Choose the best answer.

1. African Americans account for about what percentage of the population of the United States?
   - (A) 50 percent
   - (B) 30 percent
   - (C) 15 percent
   - (D) 5 percent

2. Which of the following groups has had the least amount of influence on the music, art, food, religion, and language in the United States?
   - (F) Australlans
   - (G) Africans
   - (H) Native Americans
   - (J) Europeans

3. The dominant religion in the United States is _____ .
   - (A) Judaism
   - (B) Christianity
   - (C) Islam
   - (D) Buddhism

4. Which group's influence is especially evident in the southwestern United States?
   - (F) French
   - (G) Italians
   - (H) Spanish
   - (J) Germans

5. Jazz, an American music form, has its roots in _____ .
   - (A) African music
   - (B) Native American music
   - (C) Spanish music
   - (D) French music

6. In which of the following cities would you be most likely to hear Spanish being spoken?
   - (F) Concord, New Hampshire
   - (G) Miami, Florida
   - (H) St. Paul, Minnesota
   - (J) Portland, Maine

7. *Connecticut, Illinois,* and *Mississippi* are place names that show the influence of _____ .
   - (A) French settlers
   - (B) Spanish settlers
   - (C) Native Americans
   - (D) African Americans

8. The Cajuns in Louisiana speak a dialect of _____ .
   - (F) Spanish
   - (G) French
   - (H) German
   - (J) Iroquois

STOP

Social Studies
| 1.0 |

Comparing
Cultural Characteristics
Culture

DIRECTIONS: Examine the table below. Then, answer the questions on the next page.

Country	Age Structure (% of population by age group)	Life Expectancy at Birth	Literacy Rate
Brazil	0–14 years: 25.8% 15–64 years: 68.1% 65 years and over: 6.1%	Total population: 71.97 years Male: 68.02 years Female: 76.12 years	Definition: age 15 and over can read and write Total population: 86.4%
Uruguay	0–14 years: 22.9% 15–64 years: 63.9% 65 years and over: 13.3%	Total population: 76.33 years Male: 73.12 years Female: 79.65 years	Definition: age 15 and over can read and write Total population: 98%
Bolivia	0–14 years: 35% 15–64 years: 60.4% 65 years and over: 4.6%	Total population: 65.84 years Male: 63.21 years Female: 68.61 years	Definition: age 15 and over can read and write Total population: 87.2%
Guyana	0–14 years: 26.2% 15–64 years: 68.6% 65 years and over: 5.2%	Total population: 65.86 years Male: 63.21 years Female: 68.65 years	Definition: age 15 and over has ever attended school Total population: 98.8%
United States	0–14 years: 20.4% 15–64 years: 67.2% 65 years and over: 12.5%	Total population: 77.85 years Male: 75.02 years Female: 80.82 years	Definition: age 15 and over can read and write Total population: 99%
Canada	0–14 years: 17.6% 15–64 years: 69% 65 years and over: 13.3%	Total population: 80.22 years Male: 76.86 years Female: 83.74 years	Definition: age 15 and over can read and write Total population: 99%
Belize	0–14 years: 39.5% 15–64 years: 57% 65 years and over: 3.5%	Total population: 68.3 years Male: 66.43 years Female: 70.26 years	Definition: age 15 and over can read and write Total population: 94.1%

GO

1. **When someone is born in the United States, how many years are they expected to live, based on the national average?**

    (A) 77.85 years

    (B) 65.86 years

    (C) 80.22 years

    (D) 68.3 years

2. **Which of the following countries has the greatest percentage of people aged 14 or younger?**

    (F) Canada

    (G) Belize

    (H) Brazil

    (J) United States

3. **How is the literacy rate for Guyana measured differently than the rate for the other countries in the table?**

    (A) Guyanans are defined as literate if they can read.

    (B) Guyanans are defined as literate if they can both read and write.

    (C) Guyanans are defined as literate if they can write.

    (D) Guyanans are defined as literate if they ever attended school.

4. **Of the countries shown in the table, which has the greatest percentage of people who can read and write?**

    (F) Brazil

    (G) United States

    (H) Uruguay

    (J) Belize

5. **Of the countries shown in the table, which ones have the shortest life expectancy for men?**

    (A) Belize and Bolivia

    (B) Uruguay and Brazil

    (C) Bolivia and Guyana

    (D) Canada and the United States

6. **Based on the information in the table, which of the following statements about life expectancy is probably true?**

    (F) Most Americans can expect to live well into their late 80s.

    (G) Latin American women can expect to live longer than Latin American men.

    (H) Life expectancy in Canada is dramatically lower than it is in the United States.

    (J) Overall, life expectancy in Latin America is a bit higher than it is in the United States and Canada.

7. **Which country has a life expectancy of 68.61 years for females?**

    (A) Brazil

    (B) Bolivia

    (C) Uruguay

    (D) Belize

STOP

Social Studies

2.0

Matching Events
to Historical Stories
Time, Continuity, and Change

DIRECTIONS: The following passages were written about actual events in American history. Match the selection with the correct event.

A I am tired of fighting. Our chiefs are killed. Looking Glass is dead. Toohulhulsote is dead. The old men are all dead. It is the young men who say yes or no. . . . Hear me, my chiefs. I am tired. My heart is sick and sad. From where the sun now stands I will fight no more forever.

B Listen, my children, and you shall hear
Of the midnight ride of Paul Revere,
On the eighteenth of April, in Seventy-five;
Hardly a man is now alive
Who remembers that famous day and year.

C I then shouted into M [the mouthpiece] the following sentence: "Mr. Watson—Come here—I want to see you." To my delight he came and declared that he had heard and understood what I said.

D Close behind the first gang come the [other workers] and a lively time they make of it. It is a grand Anvil Chorus that these sturdy sledges [hammers] are laying across the Plains; it is in triple time, three strokes to a spike. There are ten spikes to a rail, four hundred rails to a mile, eighteen hundred miles to San Francisco.

E But O heart! heart! heart!
O the bleeding drops of red,
Where on the deck my Captain lies,
Fallen cold and dead.

F I was really aware, visually aware, that the moon was in fact a sphere, not a disk. It seemed almost as if it were showing us its roundness, its similarity in shape to our earth, in a sort of welcome. I was sure then that it would be a hospitable host. It had been awaiting its first visitors for a long time.

_____ **1. Workers build the transcontinental railroad that links the East and West Coasts of the United States.**

_____ **2. The British march on Concord, Massachusetts, at the beginning of the American Revolution.**

_____ **3. Neil Armstrong prepares to land on the moon.**

_____ **4. Chief Joseph of the Nez Perce Indian nation surrenders to the U.S. Army.**

_____ **5. Abraham Lincoln is assassinated.**

_____ **6. Alexander Graham Bell invents the telephone.**

Social Studies

2.0

Different Perspectives on Historical Events
Time, Continuity, and Change

DIRECTIONS: The passages below are from the speeches made by Abraham Lincoln, president of the United States, and Jefferson Davis, president of the Confederacy, at their inaugurations near the start of the Civil War. Read the passages and then answer the questions that follow.

> "One section of our country believes slavery is *right* and ought to be extended, while the other believes it is *wrong* and ought not to be extended. This is the only substantial dispute. . . .
> Physically speaking, we cannot separate. We cannot remove our respective sections from each other nor build an impassable wall between them. . . .
> In *your* hands, my dissatisfied fellow countrymen, and not in *mine*, is the momentous issue of civil war."
>
> —Abraham Lincoln, March 4, 1861

> "As a necessity, not a choice, we have resorted to the remedy of separation, and henceforth our energies must be directed to the conduct of our own affairs, and the [continuation] of the Confederacy which we have formed. If a just perception of mutual interest shall permit us peaceably to pursue our separate political career, my most earnest desire will have been fulfilled. But if this be denied to us . . . [we will be forced] to appeal to arms. . . ."
>
> —Jefferson Davis, February 18, 1861

1. **According to Lincoln, the only "substantial dispute" between the North and the South was _____ .**
   - (A) the desire for war
   - (B) the issue of slavery
   - (C) the issue of states' rights
   - (D) Jefferson Davis's presidency

2. **In his speech, Davis says that separation _____ .**
   - (F) was a choice that Southerners made
   - (G) was a necessity for the South
   - (H) was physically impossible
   - (J) would lead to war

3. **When Lincoln calls Southerners "my dissatisfied fellow countrymen," it shows that _____ .**
   - (A) he considered the South a separate country
   - (B) he recognized the right of the Southern states to secede
   - (C) he felt that the South was still part of the United States
   - (D) he believed separation would solve the problem of slavery

4. **In their speeches, both Lincoln and Davis say that they _____ .**
   - (F) believe in the right to secede
   - (G) believe in the necessity of slavery
   - (H) wish to remain president
   - (J) do not wish for war

STOP

Name _____ Date _____

Using a Map
People, Places, and Environments

DIRECTIONS: Use the map below to choose the best answer.

Desert
Grassland
Tropical rain forest
Temperate rain forest
Temperate deciduous forest
Taiga
Tundra

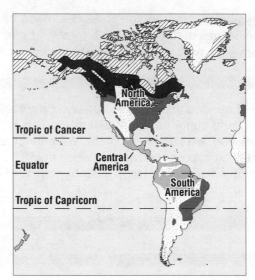

1. The Inuit are native people who live in the far north. Which types of environments do the Inuit mostly live in?

    Ⓐ taiga and tundra

    Ⓑ desert and grassland

    Ⓒ tundra and tropical rain forest

    Ⓓ taiga and temperate deciduous forest

2. Which type of environment runs north to south in the eastern United States?

    Ⓕ desert

    Ⓖ temperate deciduous forest

    Ⓗ tundra

    Ⓙ tropical rain forest

3. Tropical rain forests are found _____ .

    Ⓐ near the equator

    Ⓑ throughout much of North America

    Ⓒ in the southernmost part of South America

    Ⓓ in the far north

4. Which type of environment does Central America have?

    Ⓕ tropical rain forest

    Ⓖ desert

    Ⓗ grassland

    Ⓙ temperate rain forest

5. What are the two main types of environments in the western half of the United States?

    Ⓐ taiga and tundra

    Ⓑ tropical rain forest and desert

    Ⓒ desert and grassland

    Ⓓ taiga and temperate deciduous forest

6. Which type of environment is not found in South America?

    Ⓕ tropical rain forest

    Ⓖ desert

    Ⓗ temperate deciduous forest

    Ⓙ taiga

STOP

Social Studies

3.0

Effect of Human Activity on the Environment

People, Places, and Environments

DIRECTIONS: Choose the best answer.

1. **When soil erosion occurs, _____ .**

   Ⓐ soil washed into a river or stream can block the sunlight and slow the growth of plants in the river or stream

   Ⓑ farmlands can become less productive over time

   Ⓒ fertile topsoil is lost

   Ⓓ all of the above

2. **All of the following are attempts by people to improve the quality of water environments except _____ .**

   Ⓕ facilities that treat the water

   Ⓖ widespread use of fertilizers that are filled with harmful chemicals

   Ⓗ laws that prevent people from using wetlands

   Ⓙ restrictions on things that cause pollution

3. **Which of the following statements about acid rain is not true?**

   Ⓐ It is a type of pollution in which chemicals fall back to Earth as precipitation.

   Ⓑ It is caused by emissions from automobiles and industries.

   Ⓒ It is harmful to plants but benefits fish and other aquatic life.

   Ⓓ It damages forests.

4. **Tropical rain forests, which are home to millions of species of plants and animals, are in danger because of _____ .**

   Ⓕ logging

   Ⓖ mining

   Ⓗ slash-and-burn agriculture

   Ⓙ all of the above

DIRECTIONS: Read the following passage and then answer questions 5 and 6.

Human beings living in an area killed all the native timber wolves. The wolves were the natural predators of white-tailed deer. Over time, the deer population grew. The available plant life could not support the increased deer population. As a result, thousands of deer died of starvation.

5. **Based on the above passage, which of the following statements do you think is true?**

   Ⓐ Human activity never affects the animal population.

   Ⓑ The loss of one species from an ecosystem can lead to the overpopulation or extinction of other species.

   Ⓒ Human activity usually affects only one species in an environment.

   Ⓓ The deer in this ecosystem would have died out anyway.

6. **What is one way human beings in this ecosystem could help reduce the number of deer that die of starvation?**

   Ⓕ bring timber wolves back into the ecosystem

   Ⓖ allow controlled hunting of deer

   Ⓗ both F and G

   Ⓙ neither F nor G

STOP

Social Studies

1.0–3.0

For pages 81–87

Mini-Test 1

**Culture; Time, Continuity, and Change;
People, Places, and Environments**

DIRECTIONS: Use the map to help you answer questions 1 and 2.

1. **What do the dots on the map indicate?**

    (A) the Missouri River

    (B) the border between the Louisiana territory and Canada

    (C) the route Lewis and Clark took during their expedition of the territory

    (D) the border between the land the U.S. purchased and the land still owned by France

2. **Based on the map, which of the following countries have had an influence on the history and culture of North America?**

    (F) Great Britain

    (G) France

    (H) Spain

    (J) all of the above

DIRECTIONS: Choose the best answer.

3. **Which of the following statements about Abraham Lincoln and Jefferson Davis is true?**

    (A) Both were presidents of the United States.

    (B) Both believed that the South had the right to secede.

    (C) Both said they did not want war.

    (D) all of the above

4. **Acid rain, soil erosion, and water treatment facilities show that _____ .**

    (F) human beings can have a major impact on the environment

    (G) the actions of human beings always harm the environment

    (H) plants are rarely affected by human activity

    (J) no restrictions are needed on industrial pollution

Name _____ Date _____

Influences on Values
Individual Development and Identity

DIRECTIONS: Think about what a perfect day would be like for you. Then, answer the questions below.

1. Write a paragraph describing what that perfect day would be like. What activities would you do, what foods would you eat, and with whom would you spend time?

_____

_____

_____

_____

_____

_____

_____

2. Values are an individual's Ideas about what is right and wrong and what is important in life. What does your description of your perfect day tell about your values?

_____

_____

_____

_____

_____

3. Who or what has been the most important influence on your values?

_____

_____

_____

_____

_____

STOP

Social Studies
4.0

Regional Influences on Identity
Individual Development and Identity

DIRECTIONS: Read the passage below and then answer the questions that follow.

People from each part of the United States have special foods that help make that region unique. For example, in the Great Plains region, lefse is a popular favorite. Lefse is a soft flatbread made from potatoes, milk, and flour. It looks a little like a tortilla. Scandinavian immigrants to the Great Plains brought the recipe with them to America.

1. **Find a recipe for a dish that is closely identified with the region of the country in which you live. What is the dish called, and what are the ingredients? Is this dish a favorite of yours? Why or why not?**

_____

_____

_____

_____

2. **What foods or dishes do you and your family regularly eat that your friends do not?**

_____

_____

3. **What special foods does your family cook at special times, such as birthdays or holidays? For example, some people have sweet potato pie every Thanksgiving. Describe the preparations you and your family make.**

_____

_____

4. **How would you feel if your family did not have the special food you mentioned in question 3? How do you think preparing and eating these foods contribute to family unity and tradition?**

_____

_____

5. **Do you think you will continue to eat the foods your family eats when you are an adult? Why or why not?**

_____

STOP

Name _____ Date _____

Major Religions of the World and the United States

Individuals, Groups, and Institutions

DIRECTIONS: Use the graphs below to answer the questions.

Major Religions of the World

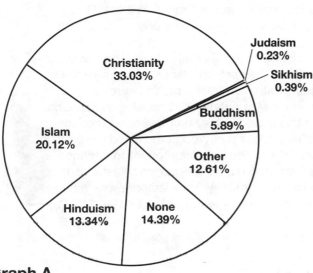

Graph A

Major Religions of the United States

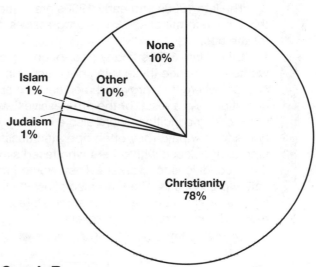

Graph B

1. **What does Graph B show?**

   (A) the number of people in the United States

   (B) the number of people in the world

   (C) the percentage of people in the world who practice certain religions

   (D) the percentage of people in the United States who practice certain religions

2. **What religion do about 20 percent of the people in the world practice?**

   (F) Islam

   (G) Hinduism

   (H) Judaism

   (J) Christianity

3. **What percentage of people in the United States practice no religion?**

   (A) 78%

   (B) 33%

   (C) 10%

   (D) 1%

4. **Which statement is supported by the information in the graphs?**

   (F) More people practice Christianity than any other religion.

   (G) Most people in the world practice Islam.

   (H) Buddhism is practiced by about six percent of the people in the United States.

   (J) Most people in the world do not practice a religion.

STOP

Social Studies

[5.0]

Social Changes in the Progressive Era
Individuals, Groups, and Institutions

DIRECTIONS: Read the passage below about the Progressive era in the United States and then answer the questions that follow.

The late 1800s and early 1900s are sometimes referred to as the *Progressive era.* During this time, reformers, known as *progressives,* fought to improve living and working conditions for the poor.

By the late 1800s, many poor people lived in crowded housing in city slums. Progressives worked to change these living conditions. In some cities, they set up places, called *settlement houses,* where they provided medical care and worked with slum residents to improve conditions. As a result of the progressives' work, many states established housing regulations.

Working conditions were also a problem during this time. Factory employees worked long hours for low pay. They often operated unsafe machinery. Workers who complained were often fired and replaced with others who faced similar conditions. Progressives fought to change these conditions for workers. They worked to pass laws that required factories to establish safety precautions. The laws also allowed workers to collect money from factory owners for injuries received on the job. In some states, progressives were able to get laws passed that required minimum pay for workers.

1. How did progressives improve conditions for factory workers?

_____

_____

_____

_____

2. Why did progressives set up settlement houses in some cities?

_____

_____

_____

_____

3. What conditions or issues do you think need to be addressed in your community today?

_____

_____

_____

_____

STOP

Name _____   Date _____

Social Studies

4.0–5.0

For pages 89–92

**Individual Development and Identity;
Individuals, Groups, and Institutions**

DIRECTIONS: Use the graph below to answer questions 1 and 2.

Major Religions of Canada

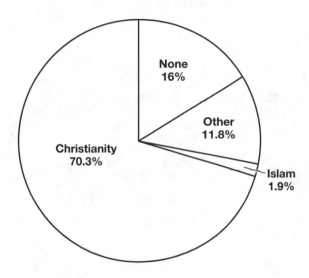

None
16%

Other
11.8%

Christianity
70.3%

Islam
1.9%

1. **What percentage of people in Canada practice Islam?**

   (A) 0%

   (B) 1.9%

   (O) 11.8%

   (D) 16%

2. **Based on the graph above and what you know about religions in the United States, which of the following statements is not true?**

   (F) Christianity is the predominant religion in both the United States and Canada.

   (G) Many people in the United States and Canada practice no religion.

   (H) Islam is practiced by a small percentage of the population in both the United States and Canada.

   (J) The practice of religion in the United States and Canada is exactly the same.

DIRECTIONS: Choose the best answer.

3. **Which of the following best describes the reformers of the Progressive era?**

   (A) people who fought for better working and living conditions for the poor

   (B) people who supported business progress

   (C) people who supported the rights of factory owners

   (D) people who believed in progressing westward

4. **Which of the following can be an influence on the values a person has?**

   (F) family

   (G) religion

   (H) society

   (J) all of the above

5. **List at least three ways that the region where you live has influenced who you are.**

   _____

   _____

   _____

   _____

   _____

   _____

   _____

   _____

   _____

   _____

STOP

Social Studies

| 6.0 |

The Federal System in the United States
Powers, Authority, and Governance

DIRECTIONS: The U.S. Constitution created a federal system that divided powers between the federal, or national, government and state governments. The Venn diagram below shows how the powers are divided. Use the Venn diagram to answer the questions that follow.

Federal Government

- Regulating trade between nations and among states
- Providing a military force
- Declaring war
- Coining money
- Setting up federal courts
- Conducting foreign affairs

Both Federal and State Governments

- Collecting taxes
- Borrowing money
- Spending funds for the general welfare of the public
- Setting up courts
- Making and enforcing laws

State Government

- Regulating trade within the state
- Setting up county and city governments
- Conducting elections
- Establishing public schools

1. **Which is a power that only the federal government has?**

   (A) coining money

   (B) borrowing money

   (C) conducting elections

   (D) setting up city governments

2. **Both the federal and state governments have the power to _____ .**

   (F) conduct foreign affairs

   (G) declare war

   (H) establish schools

   (J) collect taxes

3. **What branches of both the federal and state governments make laws? Enforce laws?**

   _____

   _____

   _____

   _____

   _____

   _____

   _____

   _____

   _____

STOP

Name _____ Date _____

Social Studies

The President's Cabinet
Powers, Authority, and Governance

DIRECTIONS: The executive branch of the U.S. government carries out the laws that Congress passes to meet the needs of the American people. The president, who is the head of the executive branch, appoints a group of advisers to help carry out the job of the executive branch. These advisers are known as the *cabinet.* They are the heads of 15 executive departments. The chart below shows the cabinet departments and their functions. Use the chart to answer the questions that follow.

Cabinet Departments	
Department of State Carries out the nation's foreign policy	**Department of Health and Human Services** Cares for the health and welfare of Americans
Department of the Treasury Deals with the nation's money—collects taxes, spends and prints money	**Department of Labor** Supervises working conditions of workers in the United States
Department of Defense In charge of the nation's military	**Department of Justice** In charge of law enforcement
Department of Housing and Urban Development In charge of housing and issues facing cities	**Department of Transportation** Manages highways, air traffic, railroads, and ocean traffic
Department of the Interior Manages the nation's public lands and natural resources	**Department of Agriculture** In charge of issues related to farms and farm products
Department of Energy In charge of the nation's energy policies	**Department of Education** Advises schools and provides funding
Department of Commerce Manages the nation's trade and businesses	**Department of Veterans Affairs** Manages services for the nation's veterans
Department of Homeland Security In charge of protecting the United States against terrorist attacks and natural disasters	

1. **Which department is in charge of the national forests in the United States?**

    (A) Department of Commerce

    (B) Department of Interior

    (C) Department of Energy

    (D) Department of Transportation

2. **What department sets up safety standards for automobiles?**

    (F) Department of Interior

    (G) Department of Energy

    (H) Department of Commerce

    (J) Department of Transportation

3. **Which of the following is a function of the Department of Justice?**

    (A) to supervise trade between the United States and other nations

    (B) to provide health care for veterans of different wars

    (C) to prosecute people who violate civil rights laws

    (D) to make sure workers work with machinery that is safe

Social Studies
7.0

Identifying Economic Systems
Production, Distribution, and Consumption

DIRECTIONS: Read the table and use it to help you answer the questions.

Type of Economic System	Definition
Traditional economy	A system in which decisions are made largely by repeating the actions from an earlier time or generation
Command economy	A system in which decisions are made largely by an authority, such as a government planning agency
Market economy	A system in which decisions are made largely by the interactions of buyers and sellers
Mixed economy	A system in which decisions are made by the market, government, and tradition

1. _____ is the way a society organizes to determine what goods and services should be produced, how they will be produced, and who will consume the goods and services.
   - (A) A government
   - (B) An economic system
   - (C) A constitution
   - (D) A trade agreement

2. The kind of economic system in which individuals own most of the stores, farms, and factories is a _____ economy.
   - (F) traditional
   - (G) command
   - (H) market
   - (J) mixed

3. The kind of economic system in which the government controls most of the stores, farms, and factories is a _____ economy.
   - (A) traditional
   - (B) command
   - (C) market
   - (D) mixed

4. An economy in which decisions are based on customs, beliefs, religion, and habits is a _____ economy.
   - (F) traditional
   - (G) command
   - (H) market
   - (J) mixed

GO

5. **In a market economy, the price of a pound of hamburger _____ .**

(A) never changes

(B) rises a little bit every year

(C) is set by the government

(D) depends on how much hamburger is available and how many people want to buy it

6. **Marcus manages an automobile factory. If he lives in a country that has a command economy, _____ .**

(F) the government will probably tell him how many cars to build this month

(G) he will decide all by himself how many cars to build this month

(H) the employees of the factory will tell him how many cars they feel like making this month

(J) he will probably examine sales figures before deciding how many cars to build this month

7. **Generally, in a command economy, the government decides _____ .**

(A) what to produce

(B) how to produce

(C) for whom to produce

(D) all of the above

8. **When an automobile manufacturer decides to charge $100,000 for its latest model car instead of $10,000, it is largely deciding which basic economic question?**

(F) What good will be produced?

(G) How will the good be produced?

(H) For whom will the good be produced?

(J) Which style of automobile will sell?

9. **Which of the following forms of government would most likely have a command economy?**

(A) a monarchy

(B) a dictatorship

(C) a republic

(D) none of the above

10. **Canada's economic system is very similar to the one in the United States. The United States has a _____ economy because both privately owned businesses and the government play important roles in making decisions about the economy.**

(F) traditional

(G) command

(H) market

(J) mixed

STOP

Social Studies

7.0

Public Goods and Services

Production, Distribution, and Consumption

DIRECTIONS: Choose the best answer.

1. **Which of the following is not a reason why government provides public goods and services?**

   (A) to promote public safety

   (B) Politicians love spending as much of the public's money as they can.

   (C) to keep people healthy

   (D) to educate citizens

2. **Public goods and services are paid for by _____ .**

   (F) taxes

   (G) library fees

   (H) the entrance fee to a city park

   (J) all of the above

3. **A type of tax where you pay an amount based on the value of your home is called a(n) _____ .**

   (A) value-added tax

   (B) property tax

   (C) income tax

   (D) sales tax

4. **A type of tax where you pay an extra amount based on the total price of items you purchase is called a(n) _____ .**

   (F) value-added tax

   (G) property tax

   (H) income tax

   (J) sales tax

5. **Which of the following is not a public service provided by your local government?**

   (A) snow removal

   (B) lawn care

   (C) street repair

   (D) police protection

6. **Which of the following is an example of government involvement in the economy?**

   (F) The Union passed an income tax during the Civil War.

   (G) The federal government created public works projects during the Depression.

   (H) Industries were converted to war production during World War II.

   (J) all of the above

DIRECTIONS: For each of the following public goods and services, write an **L** if it is provided by your local (city) government, write an **S** if it is provided by the state government, or write an **N** if it is provided by the U.S. (national) government.

_____ 7. **Post office**

_____ 8. **State patrol**

_____ 9. **Fire department**

_____ 10. **Armed forces**

_____ 11. **City parks**

_____ 12. **Sidewalk repair**

_____ 13. **Driver's license registration**

STOP

Social Studies

8.0

Inventions That Changed Society

Science, Technology, and Society

DIRECTIONS: Study the time line below and then answer the questions.

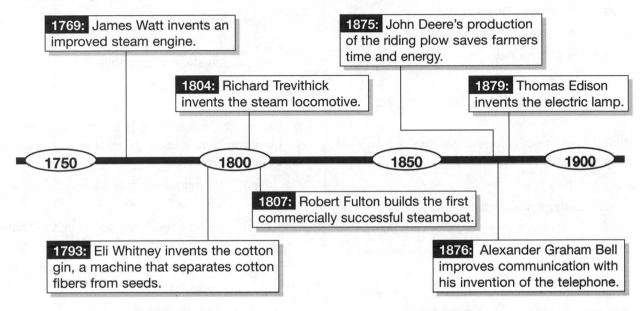

1. The above time line is a _____ source.

   (A) primary

   (B) secondary

2. Which invention was created after Fulton's steamboat was built?

   (F) the spinning jenny

   (G) the telephone

   (H) the steam engine

   (J) the cotton gin

3. How many years passed between the invention of Watt's steam engine and Edison's electric lamp?

   (A) 75

   (B) 72

   (C) 86

   (D) 110

4. Whose invention changed the way people communicated?

   (F) Richard Trevithick

   (G) Eli Whitney

   (H) Alexander Graham Bell

   (J) Robert Fulton

5. Which invention was created before Eli Whitney's cotton gin?

   (A) the steam engine

   (B) the electric lamp

   (C) the steamboat

   (D) the telephone

6. Which inventions benefited agriculture?

   (F) the cotton gin

   (G) the riding plow

   (H) the steam engine

   (J) all of the above

STOP

Social Studies

6.0–8.0

For pages 94–99

Mini-Test 3

Powers, Authority, and Governance; Production, Distribution, and Consumption; Science, Technology, and Society

1. **According to the Constitution, which is a power that only states have?**

   (A) to administer elections in the states

   (B) to coin money

   (C) to declare war

   (D) to regulate trade between nations

2. **Which kind of government has the power to levy taxes?**

   (F) state governments

   (G) federal government

   (H) both federal and state governments

   (J) neither federal nor state governments

3. **Which of the following cabinet departments is in charge of the nation's military?**

   (A) Department of Labor

   (B) Department of State

   (C) Department of Commerce

   (D) Department of Defense

4. **How does the executive branch help meet the needs of the people of the United States?**

   (F) It carries out the laws that Congress passes to meet people's needs.

   (G) It makes the laws for the nation.

   (H) It makes sure that the laws of the United States are constitutional.

   (J) It assures everyone a job and a minimum wage.

5. **Which of the following did Eli Whitney invent?**

   (A) the cotton gin

   (B) the steam engine

   (C) the steam locomotive

   (D) the riding plow

6. **Which of the following is a basic economic question that is used to determine a society's economic system?**

   (F) What goods and services should be produced?

   (G) For whom will the goods and services be produced?

   (H) How will the goods and services be produced?

   (J) all of the above

7. **An economic system in which decisions are made largely by the interactions of buyers and sellers is known as a _____ economy.**

   (A) traditional

   (B) command

   (C) market

   (D) mixed

8. **A type of tax where you pay an extra amount based on what you earn is called a(n) _____ .**

   (F) unemployment tax

   (G) property tax

   (H) income tax

   (J) sales tax

STOP

Name _____   Date _____

Social Studies

| 9.0 |

How Trade Benefits Countries
Global Connections

DIRECTIONS: Choose the best answer.

1. **Trading goods and services with people for other goods and services or money is called _____ .**

   (A) division of labor

   (B) extortion

   (C) exchange

   (D) scarcity

2. **When two people or countries trade voluntarily, _____ .**

   (F) they each have something the other one wants

   (G) they should both think they are better off after the trade than before the trade

   (H) no one forces them to make the trade

   (J) all of the above

DIRECTIONS: Read the information in the table and then answer the questions on the next page.

Country	Major Exports	Major Imports	Main Trading Partners	Currency
Brazil	transport equipment, iron ore, soybeans, footwear, coffee, autos	machinery, electrical and transport equipment, chemical products, oil	United States, Argentina, Germany	Real
Canada	motor vehicles and parts, industrial machinery, aircraft, telecommunications equipment; chemicals, plastics, fertilizers; wood pulp, timber, crude petroleum, natural gas, electricity, aluminum	machinery and equipment, motor vehicles and parts, crude oil, chemicals, electricity, durable consumer goods	United States	Canadian dollar
Honduras	coffee, shrimp, bananas, gold, palm oil, fruit, lobster, lumber	machinery and transport equipment, industrial raw materials, chemical products, fuels, foodstuffs	United States	lempira
Mexico	manufactured goods, oil and oil products, silver, fruits, vegetables, coffee, cotton	metalworking machines, steel mill products, agricultural machinery, electrical equipment, car parts for assembly, repair parts for motor vehicles, aircraft, and aircraft parts	United States	peso
United States	capital goods, industrial supplies, consumer goods, agricultural products	crude oil, consumer goods, industrial supplies, agricultural products, capital goods	Canada, Mexico, China, Japan	U.S. dollar

GO

3. **Based on the table, agricultural products _____ .**

   (A) are no longer a significant part of the United States' economy

   (B) account for very little economic activity

   (C) are a major part of the economy in most countries shown on the table

   (D) are unimportant in Latin American economies

4. **Based on the table, you can probably assume that _____ .**

   (F) the United States does not import much coffee

   (G) coffee consumption around the world is decreasing dramatically

   (H) Canada grows most of its own coffee

   (J) coffee is an important part of the economy of many Latin American nations

5. **The table reveals that Mexico is probably rich in _____ .**

   (A) silver

   (B) gold

   (C) diamonds

   (D) tin

6. **Which Latin American country is the most important trading partner for the United States?**

   (F) Brazil

   (G) Cuba

   (H) Mexico

   (J) Argentina

7. **Generally, if a country has abundant natural resources and the ability and technology to use them, _____ .**

   (A) it will be dependent on other countries to meet its needs

   (B) it will be more independent and self-sufficient in comparison to other countries

   (C) it will probably be a very poor country

   (D) it will be more likely to concentrate on just one or two economic activities in comparison to other countries

8. **The price of one country's currency measured in terms of another country's currency is known as the exchange rate. If the United States wanted to import, or purchase, oil from Mexico, the exchange rate for the U.S. dollar in Mexican _____ would need to be determined.**

   (F) dollars

   (G) lempiras

   (H) pesos

   (J) Reais

9. **Of the countries listed in the table, which one probably has the least industrialized economy? How dependent do you think this country is on its trading partners, compared to the other countries listed? Explain your answer.**

   _____

   _____

   _____

   _____

   _____

   _____

STOP

Social Studies

10.0

Freedom of Expression
Civic Ideals and Practices

DIRECTIONS: Read the passage, and then answer the questions.

First Amendment Rights

The First Amendment of the U.S. Constitution protects the civil liberties of individuals in the United States. It states: "Congress shall make no law respecting an establishment of religion, or prohibiting [forbidding] the free exercise thereof; or abridging the freedom of speech, or of the press; or the right of the people peaceably to assemble, and to petition the Government for a redress of grievances."

This amendment grants Americans the freedom of religion, or the right to practice any religion they choose. The other three freedoms are called *freedoms of expression*. The freedom of speech and the press allows people to speak or write without the government interfering. The freedom of assembly allows people to gather together for peaceful and lawful purposes. The freedom to petition guarantees people the right to ask the government to provide relief for a wrong through the courts or other governmental action.

1. **Why is it important for people in a democracy to be able to practice these freedoms?**

   _____

   _____

   _____

   _____

   _____

   _____

   _____

   _____

   _____

   _____

   _____

   _____

   _____

2. **Imagine that a new amendment was approved that took away one of these freedoms. How would that affect the way you live? What things would you no longer be able to do without this freedom?**

   _____

   _____

   _____

   _____

   _____

   _____

   _____

   _____

   _____

   _____

   _____

   _____

STOP

Social Studies
10.0

The Bill of Rights and Due Process of Law

Civic Ideals and Practices

DIRECTIONS: Choose the best answer.

1. **The first ten amendments to the U.S. Constitution are called the _____ .**

   (A) Preamble

   (B) Articles

   (C) Bill of Rights

   (D) Civil War amendments

2. **The First Amendment guarantees all of the following except _____ .**

   (F) freedom of speech

   (G) freedom of assembly

   (H) freedom of the press

   (J) the right to bear arms

3. **If you are accused of a crime, which of the following guarantees you a speedy and public trial?**

   (A) First Amendment

   (B) Second Amendment

   (C) Fourth Amendment

   (D) Sixth Amendment

4. **The Fourth Amendment guarantees that you and your property cannot be searched without a warrant. A warrant is _____ .**

   (F) an order from a judge

   (G) an order from the president

   (H) a ticket from a policeman

   (J) the same as bail money

5. **Which amendment guarantees freedom of religion?**

   (A) First Amendment

   (B) Second Amendment

   (C) Fifth Amendment

   (D) Sixth Amendment

6. **The Ninth Amendment says _____ .**

   (F) that the only rights a person has are those listed in the Bill of Rights

   (G) that people have only 10 rights

   (H) that the Bill of Rights does not list all the rights a person has

   (J) nothing about people's rights

DIRECTIONS: Read the quotes below and then answer the questions that follow.

"You have the right to remain silent. Anything you say can be used against you in a court of law. You have the right to an attorney present now and during any future questioning. If you cannot afford an attorney, one will be appointed to you free of charge if you wish."

7. **People who are in police custody must be told their rights to ensure that they do not unknowingly incriminate, or provide evidence against, themselves. This protection is guaranteed by the _____ .**

   (A) First Amendment

   (B) Fourth Amendment

   (C) Fifth Amendment

   (D) Tenth Amendment

"No person shall be . . . deprived of life, liberty, or property, without due process of law . . ."

8. **"Due process" means that _____ .**

   (F) a person's rights to life, liberty, and property can never be taken away

   (G) a person's rights cannot be taken away without a fair trial and equal protection

   (H) people must pay dues to keep their rights

   (J) people cannot be forced to pay taxes

STOP

Social Studies

9.0–10.0

For pages 101–104

Mini-Test 4

Global Connections; Civic Ideals and Practices

1. When two countries exchange goods or services for other goods and services or money, they are voluntarily participating in _____ .

   (A) division of labor

   (B) trade

   (C) extortion

   (D) a partnership

2. Not much coffee is grown in the United States. Both Colombia and Brazil grow coffee. One way for the United States to get coffee would be to _____ .

   (F) buy it from Colombia and Brazil

   (G) trade another product with Brazil for coffee

   (H) trade another product with Colombia for coffee

   (J) all of the above

3. The exchange rate is determined by comparing the value between different countries' units of _____ .

   (A) currency

   (B) investment

   (C) natural resources

   (D) labor

4. The First Amendment does not give you the right to _____ .

   (F) choose your own religion

   (G) print your ideas

   (H) make speeches

   (J) yell "fire" in a movie theater

5. The Bill of Rights is the _____ amendments to the Constitution.

   (A) first five

   (B) first 10

   (C) first 12

   (D) entire 27

6. If your house is searched without a warrant, this is a violation of your _____ rights.

   (F) First Amendment

   (G) Second Amendment

   (H) Fourth Amendment

   (J) Fifth Amendment

7. When people say that they want to "plead the Fifth," this means that they _____ .

   (A) want to exercise free speech

   (B) want to choose their religion

   (C) want a trial

   (D) choose to remain silent so that they will not incriminate themselves

8. "Due process of law" protects a person's rights to _____ .

   (F) life

   (G) liberty

   (H) property

   (J) all of the above

STOP

How Am I Doing?

Mini-Test 1

Page 88

Number Correct

4 answers correct	**Great Job!** Move on to the section test on page 108.
3 answers correct	**You're almost there!** But you still need a little practice. Review practice pages 81–87 before moving on to the section test on page 108.
0–2 answers correct	**Oops!** Time to review what you have learned and try again. Review the practice section on pages 81–87. Then, retake the test on page 88. Now, move on to the section test on page 108.

Mini-Test 2

Page 93

Number Correct

5 answers correct	**Awesome!** Move on to the section test on page 108.
4 answers correct	**You're almost there!** But you still need a little practice. Review practice pages 89–92 before moving on to the section test on page 108.
0–3 answers correct	**Oops!** Time to review what you have learned and try again. Review the practice section on pages 89–92. Then, retake the test on page 93. Now, move on to the section test on page 108.

Mini-Test 3

Page 100

Number Correct

8 answers correct	**Great Job!** Move on to the section test on page 108.
5–7 answers correct	**You're almost there!** But you still need a little practice. Review practice pages 94–99 before moving on to the section test on page 108.
0–4 answers correct	**Oops!** Time to review what you have learned and try again. Review the practice section on pages 94–99. Then, retake the test on page 100. Now, move on to the section test on page 108.

How Am I Doing?

Mini-Test 4 Page 105 **Number Correct**	**8** answers correct	**Great Job!** Move on to the section test on page 108.
	5–7 answers correct	**You're almost there!** But you still need a little practice. Review practice pages 101–104 before moving on to the section test on page 108.
	0–4 answers correct	**Oops!** Time to review what you have learned and try again. Review the practice section on pages 101–104. Then, retake the test on page 105. Now, move on to the section test on page 108.

Name _____ Date _____

Final Social Studies Test
for pages 81–104

DIRECTIONS: Examine the map of Central America below to choose the best answer.

1. **Which of the following is not a Central American country?**

   (A) El Salvador

   (B) Belize

   (C) Nicaragua

   (D) Guyana

2. **What is the capital city of Panama?**

   (F) Colón

   (G) Tegucigalpa

   (H) Panama City

   (J) San José

3. **What is another major city in Panama?**

   (A) Belize City

   (B) Managua

   (C) San José

   (D) Colón

4. **Cattle are not an important economic commodity in _____ .**

   (F) Belize

   (G) Honduras

   (H) Guatemala

   (J) Costa Rica

5. **The two most important agricultural commodities grown in El Salvador are _____ .**

   (A) bananas and coffee

   (B) sugar cane and coffee

   (C) cotton and corn

   (D) corn and sugar cane

6. **All of the following are important crops in Nicaragua except _____ .**

   (F) cotton

   (G) corn

   (H) coffee

   (J) sugar cane

DIRECTIONS: Choose the best answer.

7. **An economic system in which decisions are made by the market, government, and tradition is known as a _____ economy.**
   - (A) traditional
   - (B) command
   - (C) market
   - (D) mixed

8. **The United States has a _____ economy.**
   - (F) traditional
   - (G) command
   - (H) market
   - (J) mixed

9. **Cuba is a dictatorship, so it most likely has a _____ economy.**
   - (A) traditional
   - (B) command
   - (C) market
   - (D) mixed

DIRECTIONS: Examine the table below and then answer questions 10–12.

Name of Country	Available Resources	Needed Resources
Erehwon	bananas, coffee, coal	wheat
Utopia	coal	rice
Mythos	wheat, rice	oil
Freedonia	wheat, coffee, rice	bananas

10. **Based on the information in the table, with which country is Freedonia most likely to trade?**
    - (F) Erehwon
    - (G) Utopia
    - (H) Mythos
    - (J) Freedonia is not likely to trade with any of the other countries.

11. **One way for Erehwon to get the resources it needs would be to _____ .**
    - (A) buy them from Mythos
    - (B) trade bananas with Freedonia for them
    - (C) buy them from Freedonia
    - (D) all of the above

12. **Mythos might be unwilling to trade with any of the other countries listed because _____ .**
    - (F) Mythos has all the resources it needs
    - (G) none of them want the resources Mythos has to offer
    - (H) none of them have the oil Mythos needs
    - (J) no one in Mythos likes bananas

DIRECTIONS: Choose the best answer.

13. **The power to coin money is a power that the Constitution gives to _____ .**
    - (A) both the federal government and the state governments
    - (B) the federal government alone
    - (C) the state governments alone
    - (D) neither the federal government nor the state governments

14. **The U.S. federal government is responsible for all of the following except _____ .**
    - (F) declaring war
    - (G) maintaining water treatment plants in each American city
    - (H) negotiating treaties with other countries
    - (J) providing an army and a navy

15. **The legislative branch of both federal and state governments _____ .**
    - (A) makes laws
    - (B) enforces laws
    - (C) interprets laws
    - (D) all of the above

GO

16. **What percentage of the population of the United States is literate?**

(F) 20–39 percent

(G) 40–59 percent

(H) 60–79 percent

(J) more than 80 percent

17. **Which cabinet department helps citizens by making sure the food supply in the nation is safe?**

(A) Department of Labor

(B) Department of Commerce

(C) Department of Agriculture

(D) Department of Health and Human Services

18. **In which part of the United States is the influence of Spanish settlers most evident?**

(F) the Northeast

(G) the Midwest

(H) the Northwest

(J) the Southwest

19. **Who said: "In *your* hands, my dissatisfied fellow countrymen, and not in *mine*, is the momentous issue of civil war"?**

(A) Jefferson Davis

(B) Abraham Lincoln

(C) Robert E. Lee

(D) Ulysses S. Grant

20. **Which of the following statements about tropical rain forests is true?**

(F) They are found near the equator.

(G) They are being destroyed by fire and logging.

(H) They are home to millions of species of plants and animals.

(J) all of the above

21. **What was the main benefit of the riding plow?**

(A) It improved communication.

(B) It improved transportation.

(C) It saved farmers time and energy.

(D) It separated cotton fibers from seeds.

22. **Islam is the religion of about what percentage of the world's population?**

(F) 6%

(G) 20%

(H) 60%

(J) 80%

23. **Progressives were concerned about all of the following except _____ .**

(A) working conditions

(B) living conditions

(C) the wages people earned

(D) the rights of factory owners

24. **Which amendment to the U.S. Constitution protects civil liberties, including freedom of speech, press, and assembly?**

(F) First Amendment

(G) Second Amendment

(H) Fourth Amendment

(J) Fifth Amendment

25. **Values are an individual's ideas about _____ .**

(A) what is right and wrong

(B) what is important in life

(C) both A and B

(D) neither A nor B

STOP

Final Social Studies Test
Answer Sheet

1. (A) (B) (C) (D)
2. (F) (G) (H) (J)
3. (A) (B) (C) (D)
4. (F) (G) (H) (J)
5. (A) (B) (C) (D)
6. (F) (G) (H) (J)
7. (A) (B) (C) (D)
8. (F) (G) (H) (J)
9. (A) (B) (C) (D)
10. (F) (G) (H) (J)

11. (A) (B) (C) (D)
12. (F) (G) (H) (J)
13. (A) (B) (C) (D)
14. (F) (G) (H) (J)
15. (A) (B) (C) (D)
16. (F) (G) (H) (J)
17. (A) (B) (C) (D)
18. (F) (G) (H) (J)
19. (A) (B) (C) (D)
20. (F) (G) (H) (J)

21. (A) (B) (C) (D)
22. (F) (G) (H) (J)
23. (A) (B) (C) (D)
24. (F) (G) (H) (J)
25. (A) (B) (C) (D)

Science Standards

Standard 1—Unifying Concepts and Processes *(See pages 114–115.)*
As a result of the activities in grades K–12, all students should develop understanding and abilities aligned with the following concepts and processes:
- Systems, order, and organization.
- Evidence, models, and explanation.
- Constancy, change, and measurement.
- Evolution and equilibrium.
- Form and function.

Standard 2—Science as Inquiry *(See pages 116–117.)*
As a result of their activities in grades 5–8, all students should develop
- Abilities necessary to do scientific inquiry.
- Understandings about scientific inquiry.

Standard 3—Physical Science *(See pages 119–121.)*
As a result of their activities in grades 5–8, all students should develop an understanding of
- Properties and changes of properties in matter.
- Motion and forces.
- Transfer of energy.

Standard 4—Life Science *(See pages 122–124.)*
As a result of their activities in grades 5–8, all students should develop an understanding of
- Structure and function in living systems.
- Reproduction and heredity.
- Regulation and behavior.
- Populations and ecosystems.
- Diversity and adaptations of organisms.

Standard 5—Earth and Space Science *(See pages 125–126.)*
As a result of their activities in grades 5–8, all students should develop an understanding of
- Structure of the Earth system.
- Earth's history.
- Earth in the solar system.

Standard 6—Science and Technology *(See page 128.)*
As a result of their activities in grades 5–8, all students should develop
- Abilities of technological design.
- Understandings about science and technology.

Standard 7—Science in Personal and Social Perspectives *(See page 129.)*
As a result of their activities in grades 5–8, all students should develop an understanding of
- Personal health.
- Populations, resources, and environments.
- Natural hazards.
- Risks and benefits.
- Science and technology in society.

Science Standards

Standard 8—History and Nature of Science *(See page 130.)*
As a result of their activities in grades 5–8, all students should develop an understanding of
- Science as a human endeavor.
- Nature of science.
- History of science.

Science

1.0

Scientific Models and Patterns of Change
Unifying Concepts and Processes

DIRECTIONS: Choose the best answer.

1. **Look at the pictures below. Which is the best representation of the sun, Earth, and the Moon, overall?**

   Ⓐ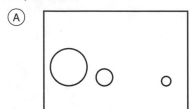

   Ⓑ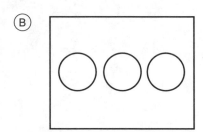

   Ⓒ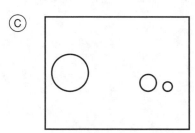

   Ⓓ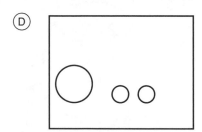

2. **Natalie is trying to explain the solar system to her younger brother. What three objects should she choose to best represent the sun, Earth, and the Moon?**

   Ⓕ a chair, a book, and a candle

   Ⓖ paper, a pencil, and a crayon

   Ⓗ a basketball, a softball, and a table tennis ball

   Ⓙ an apple, an orange, and a lemon

3. **By using these three objects to help explain a larger system, Natalie has made a _____ of the solar system.**

   Ⓐ scale

   Ⓑ model

   Ⓒ original

   Ⓓ copy

4. **The planet Venus is often called the *morning star*. This is because Venus sometimes rises above the horizon very early in the morning before sunrise. Before sunrise, Venus is often the brightest object in the sky. As the sun rises, Venus becomes fainter and fainter. Predict the day that Venus will rise at 6:00 A.M.**

Day	Time Venus Rises
Sunday	6:24 A.M.
Monday	6:20 A.M.
Tuesday	6:16 A.M.
Wednesday	6:12 A.M.
Thursday	6:08 A.M.

   Ⓕ Thursday

   Ⓖ Friday

   Ⓗ Saturday

   Ⓙ Sunday

STOP

Science

1.0

Identifying Simple Systems
Unifying Concepts and Processes

DIRECTIONS: Choose the best answer.

1. **Children are trying to get supplies up into their tree house. The simple machine which would be most useful would be a _____ .**

   (A) pulley

   (B) lever

   (C) wheel and axle

   (D) screw

2. **Which of the following simple machines makes up the base of a lightbulb?**

   (F) wheel and axle

   (G) lever

   (H) screw

   (J) pulley

3. **A bicycle contains many different simple machines. Which of the following simple maohines is the pedal assembly?**

   (A) wheel and axle

   (B) lever

   (C) screw

   (D) pulley

4. **A knife or a chisel is an example of what type of simple machine?**

   (F) an inclined plane

   (G) a lever

   (H) a wedge

   (J) a pulley

5. **A slanted surface used to raise an object is _____ .**

   (A) an inclined plane

   (B) a screw

   (C) an effort ramp

   (D) an efficiency board

6. **Which of these would not be part of an aquarium filter system?**

   (F) water

   (G) tubing

   (H) food

   (J) filter

7. **A nutcracker is an example of what type of simple machine?**

   (A) screw

   (B) wedge

   (C) pulley

   (D) lever

8. **What simple machine does not use a force, a load, and a turning point to do work?**

   (F) an inclined plane

   (G) a pulley

   (H) a lever

   (J) a screw

STOP

Science

2.0

Making Scientific Observations
Science as Inquiry

DIRECTIONS: Choose the best answer.

1. **A testable prediction is _____ .**

   (A) a hypothesis

   (B) an experiment

   (C) an exercise

   (D) a variable

2. **The process of gathering information through the senses is called _____ .**

   (F) inferring

   (G) observation

   (H) conclusion

   (J) analyzing

DIRECTIONS: Read the passages. Then, answer the questions.

Adam's Experiment

Adam wants to find out how lemon juice reacts when it is combined with different substances. In three separate paper cups, he puts equal amounts of baking soda, salt, and sugar. Then, he puts 3 drops of lemon juice into each cup. After 30 seconds, he observes all three cups.

3. **What should Adam do if he wants his lab partner to be able to repeat this experiment?**

   (A) Keep accurate records of procedures and results.

   (B) Wait until he finishes all the trials before recording any results.

   (C) Estimate the amounts of materials used.

   (D) none of these

Scott's Experiment

After discovering a moldy loaf of bread in a kitchen cabinet, Scott decided to do an experiment to determine the conditions under which mold grows the best. He suspected that mold grows best in the dark, so he put his idea to the test.

Scott bought a new loaf of bread and some sandwich bags. In each bag, he put a slice of bread, a damp paper towel, and a bit of soil. He put the bags in places that received different amounts of light, but would remain at room temperature.

In three days, Scott checked the bags. He found the most mold growing on the bread that he had put in a dark place.

4. **What was Scott's hypothesis?**

   (F) Mold grows best in a sandwich bag.

   (G) Mold will take over the world in the year 2009.

   (H) Mold grows best in the dark.

   (J) Mold grows best at room temperature.

5. **Which of the following is Scott's observation?**

   (A) He bought a new loaf of bread and some sandwich bags.

   (B) He put a slice of bread, a damp paper towel, and a bit of soil in each bag.

   (C) He put the bags in places that received different amounts of light.

   (D) He found the most mold growing on the bread that he had put in a dark place.

6. **Which of the following best explains Scott's findings?**

   (F) Light affects the growth of mold.

   (G) Temperature does not affect the growth of mold.

   (H) Mold does not need water to grow.

   (J) The sandwich bags made the mold grow.

Science

2.0

Scientific Experiments
Science as Inquiry

DIRECTIONS: Read about Ryan's experiment and then answer the questions.

Ryan wanted to find out if people could tell the difference between the taste of cold tap water and cold bottled water. He filled one glass pitcher with tap water and another glass pitcher with bottled water. Then, he placed the pitchers in the same refrigerator overnight.

1. **Before completing his experiment, Ryan guessed that people would not be able to tell the difference between the two types of water. What part of the scientific process does this guess involve?**

   (A) listing the materials

   (B) stating a hypothesis

   (C) organizing data

   (D) stating a conclusion

2. **What should be the next step in Ryan's experiment?**

   (F) He should ask several people to taste the tap water.

   (G) He should ask several people to taste the bottled water.

   (H) He should ask several people to taste both types of water and guess which one is tap water and which one is bottled water.

   (J) He should ask several people to taste both types of water and tell which one they like the best.

3. **After he has gathered the data, what should he do with it?**

   _____

   _____

   _____

   _____

   _____

   _____

   _____

4. **How can Ryan best present his findings?**

   _____

   _____

   _____

   _____

   _____

   _____

   _____

STOP

Science

1.0–2.0

For pages 114–117

Mini-Test 1

Unifying Concepts and Processes; Science as Inquiry

1. You are boiling water on your stove next to a window. You notice water droplets on the inside of the window. This is an example of what kind of scientific investigation?

   (A) observation

   (B) experimentation

   (C) collecting specimens for analysis

   (D) none of these

2. Jeannie wanted to find out if cold water was more dense than warm water. She added red food coloring to a beaker of warm water and then used an eyedropper to add the warm, red water to a beaker of cold water. This is an example of what kind of scientific investigation?

   (F) observation

   (G) experimentation

   (H) collecting specimens for analysis

   (J) none of these

3. Using the information in question 2, what is Jeannie's hypothesis?

   (A) Cold water is more dense than warm water.

   (B) Red water is more dense than clear water.

   (C) Red water is less dense than clear water.

   (D) Red food coloring makes water warmer.

4. Rollerblades are an example of what type of simple machine?

   (F) a wheel and axle

   (G) an inclined plane

   (H) a wedge

   (J) a pulley

5. A skateboarding ramp is an example of _____ .

   (A) a screw

   (B) an inclined plane

   (C) a wedge

   (D) a wheel and axle

6. Study the table below. Predict which season the southern hemisphere will have during the month of September.

Month	Northern Hemisphere	Southern Hemisphere
December	Winter	Summer
March	Spring	Autumn
June	Summer	Winter
September	Autumn	?

   (F) autumn

   (G) winter

   (H) summer

   (J) spring

7. It is important for scientists to keep accurate and detailed records so _____ .

   (A) they can decide which scientists they want to work with on future projects

   (B) they can decide who the best scientist is

   (C) more scientists can have jobs

   (D) the experiments can be repeated and the results verified

STOP

Science

3.0

Physical and Chemical Changes

Physical Science

DIRECTIONS: Choose the best answer.

1. **What characteristic best describes what happens during a physical change?**

   (A) composition changes

   (B) composition stays the same

   (C) form stays the same

   (D) mass is lost

2. **Mixtures are made of substances that are _____ .**

   (F) chemically changed and can be physically separated

   (G) chemically changed and cannot be physically separated

   (H) not chemically changed and can be physically separated

   (J) not chemically changed and cannot be physically separated

3. **If sugar and sand are mixed, which of the following methods would separate the sugar and sand?**

   (A) melt the mixture in a pot

   (B) pour the mixture through a sieve

   (C) pour the mixture into water to dissolve the sugar

   (D) They cannot be separated.

4. **How can you change matter from one state to another?**

   (F) by changing its container

   (G) by adding or removing heat

   (H) by dividing it in half

   (J) by changing its volume

5. **Which of the following sentences describes a chemical change instead of a physical one?**

   (A) A copper bracelet gets twisted into a new shape.

   (B) A copper bracelet gets melted into liquid copper.

   (C) A copper bracelet turns green when it is worn.

   (D) A copper bracelet is painted red.

6. **Which of the following is an example of a physical change?**

   (F) painting a block of wood

   (G) burning charcoal

   (H) decomposing leaves

   (J) rusting nail

7. **An example of a chemical change is _____ .**

   (A) a candlestick tarnishing

   (B) an ice cube melting

   (C) making a bat out of a piece of wood

   (D) breaking a glass bottle

8. **What changes when the mass of an object increases while volume stays the same?**

   (F) length

   (G) width

   (H) density

   (J) height

STOP

Science
3.0

Changes in
Physical Properties
Physical Science

DIRECTIONS: Choose the best answer.

1. Darion is boiling some soup in a pot. He notices that when he takes the lid off the pot, drops of water are clinging to the inside of the lid. The lid was dry when he first put it on the pot. How did the water get from the pot to the inside of the lid?

   (A) It froze there and melted.

   (B) It melted and evaporated.

   (C) It evaporated and condensed.

   (D) It melted and evaporated.

2. Jose got a helium-filled balloon at the circus on Saturday night. Inside the warm tent, his balloon was big and taut. But while he was walking to the car to go home, his balloon started to shrink. By the time he got to the car, the balloon was almost limp. What caused the balloon to shrink?

   (F) The air temperature was hotter outside the tent than inside.

   (G) The air temperature was cooler outside the tent than inside.

   (H) The temperature was the same, but the air pressure was lower outside.

   (J) The temperature was the same, but the air pressure was lower inside.

3. Which of the following properties is dependent on the size of the sample?

   (A) density

   (B) melting point

   (C) volume

   (D) solubility

4. Jaime dropped a glass bottle. It shattered into many pieces when it hit the ground. What caused the glass to break?

   (F) The ground pushed back on the glass with enough force to break the glass.

   (G) The glass lost heat and became fragile when it fell through the air.

   (H) The force of gravity caused the chemical change that made the glass weak.

   (J) The glass vibrated as it fell through the air and the vibration caused it to break.

5. Malcolm left a cube of ice in a glass on a windowsill. In about an hour, the ice changed into a clear substance that took on the shape of the lower part of the glass. Finally, after three days, there appeared to be nothing in the glass at all. What states of matter did the ice cube pass through?

   (A) liquid then gas then solid

   (B) solid then liquid then gas

   (C) gas then liquid then solid

   (D) solid then gas then liquid

6. Jerome wanted to make breakfast. First, he cracked several eggs into a bowl and stirred them briskly. Second, he grated low-fat cheese into the bowl. Third, he ground fresh black pepper into the bowl. After stirring the contents of the bowl, Jerome emptied it into a hot skillet and cooked the ingredients to perfection. Which of the steps is not a physical change?

   (F) cracking eggs into a bowl

   (G) grating the cheese

   (H) grinding the black pepper

   (J) cooking the eggs

Science
3.0

Force and Motion
Physical Science

DIRECTIONS: Choose the best answer.

1. Sandra and Dot were trying out their new skateboards. On level ground, Sandra stood on top of her skateboard, waiting for it to move. Finally, Dot pushed her. Sandra kept rolling even after Dot stopped pushing. She rolled until her skateboard hit the curb. Then, the skateboard stopped, but Sandra sailed into the grass. She was wearing her helmet and pads, so she was not hurt. Dot told her that her actions demonstrated inertia. What did Dot mean by inertia?

   (A) The curb had more friction than the skateboard, and Sandra had more friction than the grass.

   (B) Sandra could not move until something moved her, and she could not stop until something stopped her.

   (C) Sandra started moving because of gravity, and she stopped moving because of magnetism.

   (D) Sandra started moving because of kinetic energy and she stopped moving because of potential energy.

2. When an apple falls from a tree, what force causes it to land on the ground?

   (F) gravity

   (G) magnetism

   (H) inertia

   (J) friction

3. Moving something across ice instead of a gravel road is a way of _____ .

   (A) increasing friction

   (B) reducing gravity

   (C) reducing friction

   (D) increasing gravity

4. A push or pull on an object is called _____ .

   (F) work

   (G) force

   (H) mass

   (J) friction

5. Twin sisters Didi and Pati are riding bicycles home from school. Their bicycles are exactly alike except that Didi's is red and Pati's is blue. Today, it is Pati's turn to carry their schoolbooks in her backpack. When they start pedaling, Pati has to pedal harder than Didi just to keep up with Didi. When they both apply their brakes at the same time, Pati skids just a little farther than Didi. What causes these differences?

   (A) Pati has more inertia than Didi because of the schoolbooks.

   (B) Pati has more friction than Didi because of her blue bicycle.

   (C) Didi has more inertia than Pati because of her red bicycle.

   (D) Didi has more inertia than Pati because of the schoolbooks.

STOP

Name _____ Date _____

Identifying Roles
of Organisms
Life Science

DIRECTIONS: Identify each organism by writing *producer, consumer,* or *decomposer* in the blank following its name.

A **producer** is an organism that can make its own food. A **consumer** is an organism that lives by feeding on other organisms. A **decomposer** is an organism that feeds on the remains of other organisms. The unique role of an organism in its community is its **niche**.

1. cactus _____

2. lion _____

3. bacteria _____

4. cow _____

5. blue whale _____

6. grass _____

7. earthworm _____

8. fir tree _____

9. peregrine falcon _____

10. algae _____

11. palm tree _____

12. fungus _____

13. pike _____

14. sword fern _____

DIRECTIONS: Answer the following question.

15. **Choose an ecosystem, such as the tundra, a rain forest, or a desert. Describe the niches filled by various organisms—producers, consumers, and decomposers—within that ecosystem. Describe any adaptations that help an organism fill its niche.**

_____

_____

_____

_____

_____

_____

_____

_____

_____

_____

_____

_____

_____

_____

_____

STOP

Science
4.0

Adaptive Characteristics
Life Science

DIRECTIONS: Living organisms modify their environment to meet their needs. Match the need on the left with an example of how human beings have met that need.

1. _____ warmth

2. _____ food

3. _____ protection

4. _____ communication

5. _____ transportation

A. development of hunting tools

B. building fires

C. invention of cars

D. development of written language

E. building of forts

DIRECTIONS: Choose the best answer.

6. **What is an adaptation?**
   - (A) a trait or ability that helps an organism survive in its environment
   - (B) the number of pairs of genes a particular organism has
   - (C) the ways in which an organism can travel
   - (D) an organism's place in the food chain

7. **An example of an adaptation would be _____ .**
   - (F) a dog shedding its heavy coat in the summer
   - (G) the thorns on a rose bush
   - (H) a tiger's sharp teeth and claws
   - (J) all of the above

8. **One example of an adaptation in catfish is that they have dark backs and light bellies. How might this help them survive?**
   - (A) It helps them find food on the bottom of the lake.
   - (B) It helps turtles find them.
   - (C) It makes them less visible to prey from above and from below.
   - (D) It makes them taste better.

9. **Some organisms have special adaptations that help them blend into the background of their environment so that predators can't see them. This is called _____ .**
   - (F) blendability
   - (G) camouflage
   - (H) selection
   - (J) fusion

GO

DIRECTIONS: Match the ecosystem of each mystery organism in **Column A** to the adaptation that would be most beneficial for its survival in **Column B**.

COLUMN A

10. _____ in a tree in the rain forest

11. _____ underground in the backyard

12. _____ on the leaves of a rose bush

13. _____ in a coral reef

14. _____ on a glacier in Alaska

15. _____ on a mountainside

16. _____ in a polluted stream

17. _____ in the desert

18. _____ on the side of a cliff

19. _____ in a cave

20. _____ in a forest in the midwest

21. _____ on the bank of a nearly dry stream

COLUMN B

a. strong legs for climbing

b. a tail to help it hang from branches

c. deep roots to find water

d. the ability to breathe air as well as water

e. being a color that blends in with leaves

f. strong claws for digging and moving dirt

g. a thick coat and layer of fat

h. strong wings to fly and glide

i. ability to see in the dark

j. clear eyelids to keep out sand and dirt

k. hibernating in the winter when food is scarce

l. ability to completely draw inside a shell

STOP

Science
5.0

Characteristics of the Earth and Moon
Earth and Space Science

DIRECTIONS: Choose the best answer.

1. **Study the chart below and determine what the Moon phase will be during week 6.**

Ⓐ

Ⓑ

Ⓒ

Ⓓ

2. **Which is the outermost layer of Earth?**
   Ⓕ core
   Ⓖ crust
   Ⓗ mantle
   Ⓙ rim

3. **What is the source of moonlight?**
   Ⓐ reflected light from stars
   Ⓑ reflected light from moonbeams
   Ⓒ reflected light from the sun
   Ⓓ reflected light from water

4. **Earth rotates on its axis and revolves around the sun. The Moon rotates on its axis and revolves around _____ .**
   Ⓕ the sun
   Ⓖ Earth
   Ⓗ the planets
   Ⓙ the solar system

5. **Like Earth, the Moon's core is _____ .**
   Ⓐ solid rock
   Ⓑ nitrogen
   Ⓒ molten rock
   Ⓓ made up of craters

6. **The gravity of the Moon is about $\frac{1}{6}$ of the gravity on Earth. If a person weighs 120 pounds on Earth, how much would that person weigh on the Moon?**
   Ⓕ 20 pounds
   Ⓖ 60 pounds
   Ⓗ 620 pounds
   Ⓙ 720 pounds

STOP

Science
5.0

Forces Within Earth
Earth and Space Science

DIRECTIONS: Study the graph below, and then answer questions 1–4.

North Coast California: Number of Earthquakes per Year

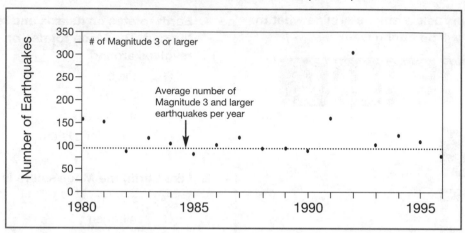

1. **In which year did the greatest number of earthquakes occur?**
    - (A) 1990
    - (B) 1991
    - (C) 1992
    - (D) 1993

2. **In which year did the fewest number of earthquakes occur?**
    - (F) 1981
    - (G) 1986
    - (H) 1991
    - (J) 1996

3. **Based on the data, what is an average number of earthquakes per year on the north coast of California?**
    - (A) about 250
    - (B) about 150
    - (C) about 100
    - (D) about 50

4. **An earthquake is caused by an abrupt shift in Earth along a fracture, or _____ .**
    - (F) fault
    - (G) seismic wave
    - (H) Geiger counter
    - (J) plate

DIRECTIONS: Choose the best answer.

5. **Igneous rocks are formed _____ .**
    - (A) from magma that has cooled
    - (B) by the accumulation of dead material
    - (C) in layers
    - (D) in ocean beds

6. **What part of Earth lies just below the crust?**
    - (F) the core
    - (G) the mantle
    - (H) the oceans
    - (J) the faults

STOP

Science

3.0–5.0

For pages 119–126

Mini-Test 2

Physical Science; Life Science; Earth and Space Science

DIRECTIONS: Choose the best answer.

1. **When water freezes, it changes from a _____ .**
   - (A) gas to a solid
   - (B) liquid to a gas
   - (C) liquid to a solid
   - (D) solid to a gas

2. **Which is an example of a physical change?**
   - (F) metal rusting
   - (G) silver tarnishing
   - (H) water boiling
   - (J) paper burning

3. **Which is an example of a chemical change?**
   - (A) ice cream melting in the sun
   - (B) crushing a soda can
   - (C) mixing salt and sugar
   - (D) burning wood in the fireplace

4. **A trait or ability that helps an organism survive in its environment is called a(n) _____ .**
   - (F) response
   - (G) adaptation
   - (H) ecosystem
   - (J) niche

5. **An example of camouflage is _____ .**
   - (A) a tiger's stripes
   - (B) a bird's beak
   - (C) a porcupine's quills
   - (D) a monkey's tail

6. **Rocks that are formed from magma that has cooled and hardened are called _____ .**
   - (F) metamorphic
   - (G) sedimentary
   - (H) conglomerate
   - (J) igneous

7. **The core is _____ .**
   - (A) the innermost layer of Earth
   - (B) the outermost layer of Earth
   - (C) the layer just below the crust
   - (D) the layer just above the mantle

8. **Sheep are examples of _____ .**
   - (F) producers
   - (G) consumers
   - (H) decomposers
   - (J) carnivores

9. **What force causes a hit baseball to fall to the ground?**
   - (A) friction
   - (B) gravity
   - (C) inertia
   - (D) magnetism

STOP

Science
6.0

Conservation, Technology, and Ecosystems
Science and Technology

DIRECTIONS: Choose the best answer.

1. **The best example of a way to conserve natural resources is _____ .**
   (A) regulating toxic emissions from cars
   (B) the greenhouse effect
   (C) cutting down on packaging used in consumer goods
   (D) keeping garbage dumps away from residential areas

2. **Which of the following is not a good soil conservation practice?**
   (F) planting trees to make a windbreak
   (G) using strip-cropping on sloping ground
   (H) planting crops without plowing
   (J) planting the same crop in a field every year

3. **Which of the following is not a conservation activity?**
   (A) replace
   (B) reuse
   (C) recycle
   (D) reduce

4. **An example of the opposite of reducing is over-packaging. Which of the following is an example of over-packaging?**
   (F) filling a cereal box completely
   (G) putting an item in a cardboard box, then putting that box in another box
   (H) putting foam packing material around a fragile item
   (J) packing an item in the smallest possible box

5. **Many power companies burn coal to make electricity. Some power companies burn coal that contains high amounts of an element called *sulfur*. When this coal is burned, the sulfur combines with oxygen to form a poisonous gas called *sulfur dioxide*. When the sulfur dioxide gas is released into the atmosphere, it combines with water to form a powerful chemical, called *sulfuric acid*. When it rains, the sulfuric acid returns to Earth as acid rain. How does acid rain change the environment?**
   (A) Acid rain helps clean buildings and roads.
   (B) Acid rain harms plants and animals.
   (C) Acid rain returns valuable nutrients to the soil.
   (D) Acid rain helps clean polluted water.

6. **A renewable resource can be replaced. A nonrenewable resource cannot be replaced. Which of the following is a nonrenewable source of energy?**
   (F) solar power   (H) wind power
   (G) gas power   (J) water power

7. **What can result when poor farming practices occur in areas that receive little rain?**
   (A) ice wedging
   (B) oxidation
   (C) leaching
   (D) desert formation

8. **What does no-till farming help prevent?**
   (F) leaching
   (G) crop rotation
   (H) overgrazing
   (J) soil erosion

STOP

Name _____ Date _____

Identifying Learned Traits
Science in Personal and Social Perspectives

DIRECTIONS: For each of the following, put an **L** in the blank if it is a learned trait. Leave all others blank.

1. _____ playing tennis

2. _____ skin color

3. _____ leaves on a tree

4. _____ hibernation

5. _____ reading

6. _____ petal color and flowers

7. _____ language

8. _____ cheek dimples

9. _____ straight or curly hair

10. _____ human beings building houses

11. _____ horses carrying riders

12. _____ tadpoles turning into frogs

13. **Describe some learned characteristics that you have acquired.**

_____

_____

_____

_____

_____

_____

_____

_____

_____

_____

_____

_____

_____

_____

_____

_____

STOP

Science
8.0

The Discoveries of Isaac Newton
History and Nature of Science

DIRECTIONS: Read the passage, and then choose the best answers.

Sir Isaac Newton

Sir Isaac Newton, born in 1642, was an English scientist, astronomer, and mathematician. Newton is sometimes described as "one of the greatest names in the history of human thought" because of his great contributions to mathematics, physics, and astronomy.

Newton discovered how the universe is held together through his theory of gravitation. He discovered the secrets of light and color, and he invented a new kind of mathematics, called *calculus*. Newton made these three discoveries within 18 months, from 1665 to 1667.

1. **Which of Newton's discoveries explains how the universe is held together?**

   (A) calculus

   (B) the theory of light and color

   (C) the theory of gravitation

   (D) the theory of relativity

2. **The new kind of mathematics that Newton invented is called _____ .**

   (F) physics

   (G) astronomy

   (H) gravitation

   (J) calculus

3. **Which of the following statements about Isaac Newton is true?**

   (A) We still use many of Newton's theories and discoveries today.

   (B) Because Newton lived so long ago, most of his theories are no longer valid.

   (C) Newton made important contributions in mathematics, physics, and biology.

   (D) Newton was a brilliant scientist and astronomer, but a poor mathematician.

STOP

Science

| 6.0–8.0 |

Mini-Test 3

Science and Technology; Science in Personal and
Social Perspectives; History and Nature of Science

DIRECTIONS: Choose the best answer.

1. **Trees are conserved when cardboard and newspapers are _____ .**
   - (A) hauled to a dump
   - (B) burned
   - (C) kept in storage
   - (D) recycled

2. **Walking or riding a bicycle to a store rather than having someone drive you in a car is an example of _____ .**
   - (F) replacing
   - (G) recycling
   - (H) reducing
   - (J) reusing

3. **A windbreak helps prevent _____ .**
   - (A) soil depletion
   - (B) water erosion
   - (C) wind erosion
   - (D) none of these

4. **Which of the following is a renewable source of energy?**
   - (F) oil
   - (G) wind
   - (H) coal
   - (J) gas

5. **Which of the following is an example of conserving natural resources by reusing?**
   - (A) refilling water bottles at grocery stores
   - (B) shipping items in several boxes
   - (C) buying items that have little packaging
   - (D) carpooling

6. **Which of the following is a learned trait?**
   - (F) birds laying eggs
   - (G) bees stinging
   - (H) dogs shaking hands
   - (J) the number of petals on a rose

7. **Which of the following is not a learned trait?**
   - (A) riding a bike
   - (B) counting
   - (C) playing cards
   - (D) hair color

8. **Isaac Newton made important discoveries in all of the following areas except _____ .**
   - (F) mathematics
   - (G) physics
   - (H) biology
   - (J) astronomy

STOP

How Am I Doing?

Mini-Test 1

Page 118

Number Correct

7 answers correct	**Great Job!** Move on to the section test on page 133.
5–6 answers correct	**You're almost there!** But you still need a little practice. Review practice pages 114–117 before moving on to the section test on page 133.
0–4 answers correct	**Oops!** Time to review what you have learned and try again. Review the practice section on pages 114–117. Then, retake the test on page 118. Now, move on to the section test on page 133.

Mini-Test 2

Page 127

Number Correct

8–9 answers correct	**Awesome!** Move on to the section test on page 133.
6–7 answers correct	**You're almost there!** But you still need a little practice. Review practice pages 119–126 before moving on to the section test on page 133.
0–5 answers correct	**Oops!** Time to review what you have learned and try again. Review the practice section on pages 119–126. Then, retake the test on page 127. Now, move on to the section test on page 133.

Mini-Test 3

Page 131

Number Correct

8 answers correct	**Great Job!** Move on to the section test on page 133.
5–7 answers correct	**You're almost there!** But you still need a little practice. Review practice pages 128–130 before moving on to the section test on page 133.
0–4 answers correct	**Oops!** Time to review what you have learned and try again. Review the practice section on pages 128–130. Then, retake the test on page 131. Now, move on to the section test on page 133.

Name _____   Date _____

Final Science Test
for pages 114–130

DIRECTIONS: Read about Zoe's experiment and study her graphs. Then, answer questions 1 and 2.

Zoe wanted to find out how sunlight and water affect a plant's growth. She did an experiment with three different scenarios. Plant A received both water and sunlight. Plant B received water, but no sunlight. Plant C received sunlight, but no water. Her results are graphed below.

Plant A

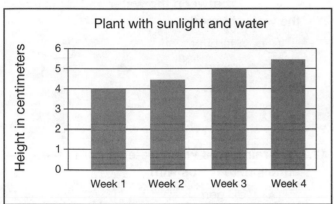

Plant B

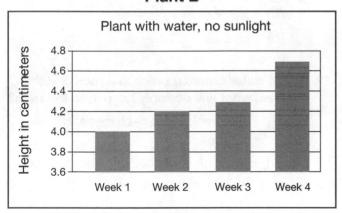

Plant C

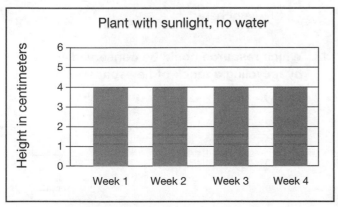

1. **Zoe might have decided to make graphs of her data because it made it easier to**
   _____ .
   - (A) keep her data organized
   - (B) compare the growth of each plant
   - (C) draw conclusions about her data
   - (D) all of the above

2. **What conclusion can Zoe draw from her experiment?**
   - (F) Plants grow best if they have water, but no sunlight.
   - (G) Plants grow best if they have sunlight, but no water.
   - (H) Plants grow best if they have both water and sunlight.
   - (J) Plants don't need water or sunlight in order to grow.

DIRECTIONS: Choose the best answer.

3. **Which of these is an example of camouflage?**
   - (A) The stick insect resembles the twig on which it sits.
   - (B) The young joey grows and develops in its mother's pouch.
   - (C) The anteater has a long, slender snout and a long tongue, which it can thrust into anthills.
   - (D) The porcupine is covered with long sharp quills.

4. **Which of these would not be found in a desert ecosystem?**
   - (F) cactus
   - (G) lizard
   - (H) otter
   - (J) tortoise

GO

5. Study the chart below. What will the moon phase probably be on March 27?

Date	Moon Phase
December 29	Full moon
January 5	Last quarter
January 11	New moon
January 19	First quarter
January 27	Full moon
February 3	Last quarter
February 10	New moon
February 18	First quarter
February 26	Full moon

(A) full moon

(B) last quarter

(C) new moon

(D) first quarter

6. Baseball pitchers use several forces to change the motion of the ball. One force is the strong push from the pitcher's arm that starts the ball moving toward home plate. What force pulls the ball down as it moves?

(F) velocity

(G) friction

(H) inertia

(J) gravity

7. When water melts from an ice cube, it is an example of a physical change. The water changes from a _____ .

(A) solid to a gas

(B) liquid to a vapor

(C) solid to a liquid

(D) liquid to solid

8. Which of these is the innermost layer of Earth?

(F) mantle

(G) core

(H) crust

(J) trench

9. Tuesday afternoon, there was a summer shower in Dallas. The next day, Josh noticed the water puddle on the sidewalk in front of his house was becoming smaller and smaller. Which of the following explains what happened to the water?

(A) It condensed.

(B) It evaporated.

(C) It melted.

(D) It froze.

10. When the wind blows across a body of water, _____ between the water and air causes the water to move.

(F) a turbine

(G) gravity

(H) friction

(J) density

11. Acid rain forms when water vapor in the atmosphere mixes with _____ .

(A) oxygen

(B) hydrogen

(C) sulfur oxides

(D) nitrogen

12. When water enters a crack in a rock and then freezes, what will possibly happen to the rock?

(F) The crack might get larger and split the rock.

(G) The rock might become stronger due to the ice.

(H) The rock might melt and change into an igneous rock.

(J) not here

13. Which resource could be conserved by recycling a stack of newspapers?

(A) rocks

(B) trees

(C) plastic

(D) oil

GO

DIRECTIONS: Read the passage and use it to answer questions 14 and 15.

Earth is a restless place. Although it may seem perfectly solid to you, the ground below your feet is moving at this very moment. The continents rest on top of the brittle crust of Earth, which has broken apart into pieces. These pieces are called *tectonic plates.* They float around on top of the molten interior of the earth, much like crackers floating in a bowl of soup. Molten rock, or lava, continues to push up through cracks in the plates. This pushes the plates even farther apart. The continents used to be closer together. Over the years, they have drifted farther apart, at the rate of about one inch every year.

14. What are tectonic plates?

- (F) molten rock
- (G) pieces of Earth's crust
- (H) cracks in Earth's surface
- (J) parts of Earth's molten core

15. According to this passage, why do tectonic plates move around?

- (A) They are floating on water.
- (B) Molten rock pushes up through the crack and pushes them apart.
- (C) The continents are reconnecting.
- (D) The crust of Earth is breaking.

DIRECTIONS: Choose the best answer.

16. Which of the following is a learned characteristic?

- (F) shoe size
- (G) height
- (H) the ability to read
- (J) the ability to roll your tongue

17. Which of the following is not a learned trait?

- (A) blinking your eyes
- (B) riding a skateboard
- (C) playing basketball
- (D) learning a language

18. If you use balls to explain the structure of a molecule, you have made _____ .

- (F) a scale
- (G) a model
- (H) an original
- (J) a copy

19. Study the table below. Which month is likely to have the most hurricanes?

Table of Tropical Storms and Hurricanes (1886–1996)		
Month Formed	**Tropical Storms**	**Hurricanes**
January–April	4	1
May	14	3
June	57	23
July	68	35
August	221	?
September	311	?
October	188	?
November	42	22
December	6	3

- (A) July
- (B) August
- (C) September
- (D) October

20. Which is an example of a chemical change?

- (F) water boiling
- (G) metal rusting
- (H) ice melting
- (J) a rock being crushed

21. Using a flagpole is an example of what simple machine?

- (A) a screw
- (B) a wedge
- (C) an inclined plane
- (D) a pulley

STOP

Final Science Test

Answer Sheet

1. (A) (B) (C) (D)
2. (F) (G) (H) (J)
3. (A) (B) (C) (D)
4. (F) (G) (H) (J)
5. (A) (B) (C) (D)
6. (F) (G) (H) (J)
7. (A) (B) (C) (D)
8. (F) (G) (H) (J)
9. (A) (B) (C) (D)
10. (F) (G) (H) (J)

11. (A) (B) (C) (D)
12. (F) (G) (H) (J)
13. (A) (B) (C) (D)
14. (F) (G) (H) (J)
15. (A) (B) (C) (D)
16. (F) (G) (H) (J)
17. (A) (B) (C) (D)
18. (F) (G) (H) (J)
19. (A) (B) (C) (D)
20. (F) (G) (H) (J)

21. (A) (B) (C) (D)

Answer Key

Pages 9–10
1. A
2. J
3. D
4. H
5. B
6. G
7. B
8. J

Pages 11–12
1. D
2. F
3. B
4. G
5. D
6. H
7. D
8. F
9. D

Pages 13–14
1. play
2. poetry
3. fable
4. B
5. H
6. A
7. J
8. B
9. J
10. myth
11. science fiction
12. realistic fiction
13. nonfiction

Page 15
1. D
2. G
3. B
4. F
5. C
6. H
7. D
8. G
9. D

Page 16
1. B
2. F
3. C
4. J
5. C
6. H

Page 17 Mini-Test 1
1. B
2. G
3. C
4. F
5. D
6. F
7. A

Page 18
1. friend—C, Jim—P, city—C
2. week—C, Jim—P, Natural History Museum—P
3. Uncle Jasper—P, Dallas Museum of Art—P
4. Jim—P, paintings—C, museum—C
5. Jim—P, Texas State Fair—P
6. fair—C, Fair Park—P, October—P
8–12. Answers will vary, but each sentence should include a proper noun.

Paragraphs will vary but should tell about a time when the student and a relative visited a special place. All common and proper nouns should be circled.

Page 19
1. have
2. attract
3. are, are
4. protect
5. have
6. climb
7. eat
8. are
9. is
10. has

The corrected verbs are: are, start, says, goes, start, is, is, gets, knows, has, get, are, means, is, don't, bites, looks, says, are, gives.

Page 20
are, is, fly, are, catch, tie, take, dive, keep, are, perch, have
1. are
2. are
3. like
4. are
5. are
6. are
7. is
8. are

Page 21
1. compound
2. simple
3. compound
4. simple
5. simple
6. compound
7. B
8. F
9. A

Page 22
1. A
2. J
3. C
4. F

Page 23
1. B
2. F
3. B
4. H

Page 24
1. 2
2. 3
3. 1
4. 3
5. 2
6. 2
7. 3
8. 1
9. 3
10. 1

Page 25
1. buy
2. cents
3. due
4. it's
5. there
6. here
7. they're
8. read
9. where
10. Proclamation, Appalachian Mountains
11. Revolutionary War, Quebec, North, Florida, South
12. Stamp Act
13. Boston Tea Party, Tea Act
14. Gadsden Purchase

Page 26
1. A
2. F
3. C
4. F
5. A
6. H
7. B
8. F
9. C

Page 27
1–8. Answers will vary. Students should rewrite the sentences using the figurative language of their choice.

Page 28 Mini-Test 2
1. C
2. J
3. C
4. They're
5. its
6. are
7. has
8. F
9. C
10. H

Page 29
1. B
2. H
3. D
4. H
5. A
6. H

Pages 30–31
1. Answers will vary. Students should define three words from the passage using an online dictionary.
2. Students' responses will vary but should reflect the research that the students did online.
3. Charles Blondin was the pseudonym of Frenchman Jean François Gravelet.

Page 32 Mini-Test 3
1. D
2. G
3. B
4. H
5. A
6. Answers will vary. Students might indicate Internet sites, science books, library books on insects, or encyclopedia articles.

Page 33
Students' responses will vary. Brief descriptions of the historical works follow.
- *Beowulf*—Old English epic poem
- Anansie tales—West Indian/ African folktales
- *The Twenty-Two Goblins*—Indian folklore series
- "The Two Frogs"—Japanese folktale
- *The Nose*—Russian short story
- *A Modest Proposal*—Irish satirical essay
- "The Animals Sick of the Plague"—French fable
- "Ode on a Grecian Urn"—English poem

Page 34
Answers will vary. In the first paragraph, students should identify three organizations. In the second paragraph, students should give reasons why they would be interested in volunteering for these organizations. In the concluding paragraph, students should explain what contributions they would make to these organizations as volunteers.

Page 35
1. Students should indicate what they believe are the effects of violence in the media.
2. Students should indicate any graphs, charts, or other statistical materials that support the topic of the composition.
3. Students should include sources to support the topic.
4. Students should provide well-thought-out solutions.

Compositions should include a clear statement of purpose. Students should define and defend their opinions with at least two supporting details. Compositions should conclude with a summary statement.

Page 36 Mini-Test 4
Paragraphs will vary. Students should identify the problem and explain why they think it is a serious problem. Students should also explain what they think world leaders could do to help solve the problem.

Pages 39–41 Final English Language Arts Test
1. B
2. F
3. C
4. F
5. C
6. H
7. C
8. G
9. A
10. H
11. A
12. J
13. B
14. F
15. C
16. H
17. A
18. J
19. B
20. H
21. A
22. H
23. B

Page 44
1. $2 \times 2 \times 5 \times 5$
2. $2 \times 3 \times 5 \times 7$
3. $2 \times 2 \times 11$
4. $2 \times 3 \times 5 \times 5 \times 7$

Page 45
1. 0.8
2. 0.375
3. 1.67
4. 0.78
5. 0.39
6. 0.07
7. 0.018
8. 1.32
9. 0.0005
10. 87%
11. 120%
12. 45%
13. 2%
14. 34.2%
15. $\frac{6}{10}$ or $\frac{3}{5}$
16. $\frac{42}{100}$ or $\frac{21}{50}$
17. $\frac{25}{1000}$ or $\frac{1}{40}$
18. $\frac{85}{100}$ or $\frac{17}{20}$
19. $\frac{192}{100}$ or $1\frac{23}{25}$

Page 46
1. B
2. H
3. D
4. G
5. B
6. G
7. C
8. G

Page 47
1. C
2. F
3. C
4. G
5. A
6. J

Page 48
1. 91
2. 34
3. 17
4. −14
5. −10
6. 16
7. 76
8. 9
9. 0
10. 1

Page 49

1. 0, 3, 6, 9, 12, 15
2. 3, 9, 15, 21, 27, 33
3. $x + 4$
4. $4x$
5. $x - 2$
6.

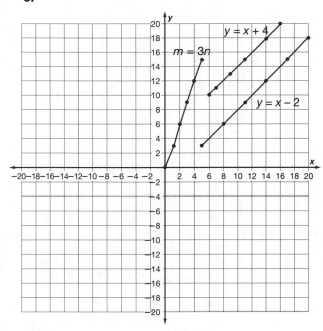

Page 50

1. A
2. H
3. B
4. H
5. B
6. G
7. B

Page 51

1. C
2. J
3. A
4. H
5. A
6. H
7. A

Page 52

1. B
2. G
3. B
4. H
5. D
6. G
7. B
8. F
9. D

Page 53

1. C
2. H
3. D
4. F
5. A

Page 54 Mini-Test 1

1. B
2. J
3. C
4. H
5. A
6. H
7. 21, 23, 25

Page 55

1. rectangle; 90°
2. parallelogram; 128°
3. square; 90°
4. trapezoid; 54°
5. trapezoid; 120°
6. parallelogram; 120°

Page 56

1. pyramid
2. prism
3. pyramid
4. prism
5. neither
6. pyramid
7. pyramid
8. prism
9. prism

Page 57

1. F = (2, 6),
   L = (5, 6),
   A = (5, 4),
   G = (5, 2)
2. B = (−2, 2),
   O = (1, 2),
   X = (1, −1),
   D = (−2, −1)
3. S = (2, −3),
   H = (2, −5),
   A = (−2, −5),
   P = (−2, −6),
   E = (−5, −6)

Page 58

1. A
2. 8 left, 2 down
3. reflection across the y-axis
4. reflection across the x-axis

Page 59

1. yes
2. yes
3. yes
4. yes
5. no
6. no

7–12.

none

Page 60

1. C
2. G
3. D
4. F
5. 180 in.³
6. 198 mm³
7. 216 m³
8. 20 in.³

Page 61

1. B
2. G
3. D
4. G
5. B
6. G
7. D
8. J

Page 62

1. C = 25.12 in.
   A = 50.24 in.²
2. C = 314 mm
   A = 7,850 mm²
3. C = 9.42 in.
   A = 7.065 in.²
4. C = 62.8 ft.
   A = 314 ft.²
5. C = 5.024 cm
   A = 2.0096 cm²
6. C = 3.14 mm
   A = 0.785 mm²
7. C = 125.6 mm
   A = 1,256 mm²
8. C = 47.1 in.
   A = 176.625 in.²
9. C = 13.188 m
   A = 13.8474 m²

Page 63

1. right 60°
2. obtuse 110°
3. obtuse 20°
4. acute 50°
5. right 50°
6. acute 71°
7. 127°

8. 75°
9. 55°
10. 105°
11. 90°
12. 115°

Page 64
1. B
2. H
3. C
4. G
5. A
6. G
7. C
8. G

Page 65 Mini-Test 2
1. reflection across y-axis
2. B
3. H
4. C
5. H
6. C
7. rectangle or square

Page 66

Math Test Scores (out of 50 points)	
Stem	Leaf
3	5, 7, 8
4	1, 3, 4, 5, 5, 7, 8, 9
5	0, 0, 0

The median grade for the math test was 45.

Page 67
1. Mean: 44.2
   Median: 45
   Mode: 45
   Range: 50
2. Mean: 48
   Median: 41
   Mode: 35
   Range: 55
3. Mean: 64.1
   Median: 60
   Mode: 85
   Range: 80
4. Mean: 62.7
   Median: 60
   Mode: 60
   Range: 56
5. Store 3 does not have the best

variety of prices. Only one brand of shoe was low, creating a large range. However, the average shoe costs $64.1 and half the shoes are over $55.
6. Store 1
7. Store 2 has the best variety of low-priced shoes. The median of $41 tells us that half the shoes cost less than $41.

Page 68
1. B
2. J
3. Students' answers will vary but should generally state that increasing the sample size (i.e., picking cards 100 times rather than 2 times) should cause Jose's prediction of the empirical probability to more closely resemble the theoretical probability of $\frac{12}{52}$.

Page 69
Students are to show probability outcomes for a number of situations. They may choose different ways to show the outcomes. Sample answers below illustrate the outcomes as tree diagrams.

1.

2.
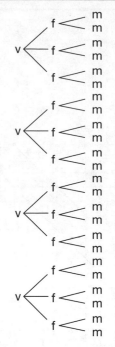

3.
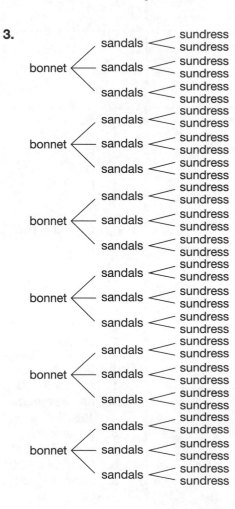

Page 70
1. C
2. H
3. D
4. F
5. B
6. H

Page 71
1. A
2. H
3. B
4. J
5. B
6. F
7. D
8. F

Page 72
1. C
2. F
3. C
4. F
5. B

Page 73
1. B
2. J
3. C
4. G
5. A
6. G
7. A

Page 74 Mini-Test 3
1. B
2. H
3.

Stem	Leaf
7	0, 4, 5, 6
8	1, 6, 9
9	2, 4, 7

4. A
5. F
6. A
7. F

Pages 76–78 Final Mathematics Test
1. D
2. H
3. B
4. J
5. B
6. F
7. B
8. H
9. A
10. F
11. B
12. J
13. B
14. H
15. C
16. H
17. A
18. G
19. B
20. J
21. B
22. H

Page 81
1. C
2. F
3. B
4. H
5. A
6. G
7. C
8. G

Pages 82–83
1. A
2. G
3. D
4. G
5. C
6. G
7. B

Page 84
1. D
2. B
3. F
4. A
5. E
6. C

Page 85
1. B
2. G
3. C
4. J

Page 86
1. A
2. G
3. A
4. F
5. C
6. J

Page 87
1. D
2. G
3. C
4. J
5. B
6. H

Page 88 Mini-Test 1
1. C
2. J
3. C
4. F

Page 89
1. Paragraphs will vary. Students should include the elements of their perfect day.
2. Answers will vary. Students should explain how the elements of their perfect day reflect their values.
3. Students' responses will vary, but students should describe who or what has influenced the values they have.

Page 90
1–5. Students' answers will vary depending on the region of the country in which they live and their personal preferences and family traditions.

Page 91
1. D
2. F
3. C
4. F

Page 92
1. They worked for laws to establish safety precautions in factories, to allow workers to collect money for work injuries, and to set up minimum wages.
2. They set up settlement houses to provide medical care and to work with slum residents to help improve their living conditions.

3. Answers will vary, but students should suggest conditions or issues in their school or community that they think need improvement.

Page 93 Mini-Test 2
1. B
2. J
3. A
4. J
5. Answers will vary, but students should list at least three ways that the region where they live has influenced their identity.

Page 94
1. A
2. J
3. The legislative branches make laws. In the federal government, this is the Congress; in most states, it is the General Assembly. The exeoutive branches enforce laws. In the federal government, the executive branch is led by the president; in the states, it is led by the governor.

Page 95
1. B
2. J
3. C

Pages 96–97
1. B
2. H
3. B
4. F
5. D

6. F
7. D
8. H
9. B
10. J

Page 98
1. B
2. J
3. B
4. J
5. B
6. J
7. N
8. S
9. L
10. N
11. L
12. L
13. S

Page 99
1. B
2. G
3. D
4. H
5. A
6. J

Page 100 Mini-Test 3
1. A
2. H
3. D
4. F
5. A
6. J
7. C
8. H

Pages 101–102
1. C
2. J
3. C
4. J
5. A
6. H
7. B
8. H
9. Honduras has the least industrialized economy. Its main exports are basic agricultural items. This makes the country very dependent on its

trading partners for many of the resources it needs.

Page 103
1. Students' paragraphs will vary but should describe how freedom of expression is important in a democracy.
2. Students' paragraphs will vary but should describe ways that their lives would be different if one of these freedoms was taken away.

Page 104
1. C
2. J
3. D
4. F
5. A
6. H
7. C
8. G

Page 105 Mini-Test 4
1. B
2. J
3. A
4. J
5. B
6. H
7. D
8. J

Pages 108–110 Final Social Studies Test
1. D
2. H
3. D
4. H
5. B
6. J
7. D
8. J
9. B
10. F
11. D

12. H
13. B
14. G
15. A
16. J
17. C
18. J
19. B
20. J
21. C
22. G
23. D
24. F
25. C

Page 114
1. C
2. H
3. B
4. H

Page 115
1. A
2. H
3. A
4. H
5. A
6. H
7. D
8. F

Page 116
1. A
2. G
3. A
4. H
5. D
6. F

Page 117
1. B
2. H
3. Ryan needs to analyze the data he collected, and then draw conclusions from the data. He should decide if the conclusions support his original hypothesis.

4. Answers will vary. Students might suggest that Ryan present his findings in graph form along with his written report.

Page 118 Mini-Test 1
1. A
2. G
3. A
4. F
5. B
6. J
7. D

Page 119
1. B
2. H
3. C
4. G
5. C
6. F
7. A
8. H

Page 120
1. C
2. G
3. C
4. F
5. B
6. J

Page 121
1. B
2. F
3. C
4. G
5. A

Page 122
1. producer
2. consumer
3. decomposer
4. consumer
5. consumer
6. producer
7. decomposer
8. producer
9. consumer
10. producer
11. producer
12. decomposer
13. consumer
14. producer

15. Answers will vary, but students should correctly describe an ecosystem, the unique organisms found within that ecosystem, the roles played by those organisms, and any related adaptations.

Pages 123–124
1. B
2. A
3. E
4. D
5. C
6. A
7. J
8. C
9. G
10. b
11. f
12. e
13. l
14. g
15. a
16. d
17. j
18. h
19. i
20. k
21. c

Page 125
1. D
2. G
3. C
4. G
5. C
6. F

Page 126
1. C
2. J
3. C
4. F
5. A
6. G

Page 127 Mini-Test 2
1. C
2. H
3. D
4. G
5. A
6. J
7. A
8. G
9. B

Page 128
1. C
2. J
3. A
4. G
5. B
6. G
7. D
8. J

Page 129
1. L
2. (blank)
3. (blank)
4. (blank)
5. L
6. (blank)
7. L
8. (blank)
9. (blank)
10. L
11. L
12. (blank)
13. Answers will vary. Students might describe any skills, hobbies, or other unique behaviors that they exhibit.

Page 130
1. C
2. J
3. A

Page 131 Mini-Test 3
1. D
2. H
3. C
4. G
5. A
6. H
7. D
8. H

Pages 133–135 Final Science Test
1. D
2. H
3. A
4. H
5. A
6. J
7. C
8. G
9. B
10. H
11. C
12. F
13. B
14. G
15. B
16. H
17. A
18. G
19. C
20. G
21. D

NOTES